I Am Near

I Am Near

A Grief Devotional for Mothers Who Have Lost a Child

Becky Hunt

Z Faith • New York

This book is designed to provide helpful information on a difficult subject. In addition to looking toward the Scripture and God, if the reader requires personal assistance or advice, a mental health professional should be consulted.

Z Faith
An imprint of Zeitgeist™
A division of Penguin Random House LLC
1745 Broadway, New York, NY 10019
zeitgeistpublishing.com
penguinrandomhouse.com

ISBN: 9798217330928
Ebook ISBN: 9798217330911

Printed in the United States of America
1st Printing

Illustrations © Shutterstock.com
Book design by Suzanne LaGasa
Author photograph © by Bailee Jeffries
Edited by Patty Consolazio and Kim Suarez

The authorized representative in the EU for product safety and compliance is
Penguin Random House Ireland, Morrison Chambers, 32 Nassau Street, Dublin D02
YH68, Ireland. https://eu-contact.penguin.ie

For Gracie, my first heartbeat of
motherhood. I carry you always,
until heaven brings us home together.

Contents

PART 2

When Faith Feels Fragile: Wrestling Honestly with God

PART 3

Who Am I Now? Motherhood in the Shadow of Loss

PART 4

Light After the Valley: Walking Toward Healing and Hope

Introduction

I never wanted to write a book like this. I never wanted to join the club that no mother wants to belong to. The one where your child's name is spoken in past tense. When my daughter died, every prayer turned into a question: *Where were you, God? How could you let this happen?*

My daughter, Gracie, was born in 2012 with a congenital heart defect and lived for 82 days. After her open-heart surgery, we were told she'd be coming home, that she'd live a long, full life. That life felt stolen from me. I was angry at God, at people, at every empty phrase meant to comfort. The world didn't know what to do with my grief, and every time someone asked, "Do you have any kids?" I froze between honesty and guilt.

This devotional was born from that space: the space between faith and fury, belief and heartbreak. It's for you, the mom who still wants to believe but doesn't know how. My hope is that these pages speak to your heart no matter what your loss looks like, whether it happened in miscarriage, stillbirth, infancy, childhood, or adulthood.

Each week, you'll find one reflection from Scripture and a prayer for each day. A rhythm of truth and tenderness for weary hearts like yours. And if you need to, you can move around this book and linger on whatever topic meets you where you are.

This isn't about fixing grief or moving on. It's an invitation to meet God in the ache, to bring him your anger and your questions, and to find that even here, his presence will not let you go.

PART 1

When the World Stops: Living in the Reality of Loss

WEEK 1

Is God Still Good When Life Is Not?

How can I trust a good God when my world has fallen apart?

In all their suffering he also suffered,
and he personally rescued them.
In his love and mercy he redeemed them.
He lifted them up and carried them
through all the years.

—**Isaiah 63:9**

When your child dies, words about God's goodness can sound hollow. You may look at what's left of your world and wonder, *If God is good, why didn't he stop this?* Goodness can feel abstract when your arms are empty.

Isaiah 63:9 gives a different picture of goodness. It tells of a God who does not watch suffering from a distance but *feels it with us.* "In all their suffering he also suffered." Every moment your heart broke, his did, too. His goodness is not proven by prevention but by presence.

God's goodness doesn't always change circumstances; it carries us through them. He lifts us when we collapse, weeps beside us when memories sting, and holds us steady when our own strength is gone. That kind of goodness doesn't erase pain; it enters it.

You don't have to pretend this loss is good. It isn't. Death was never part of God's original design for his children, and his heart breaks with yours. But even here, his mercy still reaches. His arms still carry. His love still surrounds what feels unfixable.

Sometimes his goodness looks less like rescue and more like endurance—the quiet strength that keeps you breathing when you didn't think you could survive another day.

Goodness may not feel like light right now; it may feel like breath, or survival, but it's still him, holding you through every step, promising that this darkness will not have the final word. His goodness remains, even here, even now.

DAILY PRAYERS

DAY 1 God, I can't see your goodness right now. Everything feels dark and unfair, and I'm just trying to make it through the next breath. Please carry me when I can't take another step. Wrap me in your presence and remind me, even in this heartbreak, that you are still near. Amen.

DAY 2 Lord, you suffered, too. You know what it feels like to lose, to ache, to weep over what was taken too soon. You understand pain that language can't describe. Remind me that you don't just watch from above; you enter my sorrow with me and hold me in it. Amen.

DAY 3 Father, I'm tired of trying to make sense of this. My questions don't have answers, and my faith feels fragile. Please meet me in the confusion. Give me peace that doesn't depend on understanding and faith to believe you are still who you've always been—good, loving, and near. Amen.

DAY 4 God, when memories come rushing in and I can't hold back the tears, remind me that you see every one of them. You weep with me over what's been lost. Help me rest in knowing that my pain matters to you and that your heart breaks with mine. Amen.

DAY 5 Lord, some days I'm scared to hope for anything good because everything good feels like it could be stolen from me. You show me that your goodness isn't something I have to earn or protect. Help me notice the quiet ways you're holding me together when I feel like I'm falling apart. Amen.

DAY 6 Father, sometimes I wonder if I'll ever feel joy again. Remind me that it's okay to smile without guilt and to feel light in small moments. You're not asking me to forget, only to keep breathing. Thank you for staying close while my heart slowly learns to hope again. Amen.

DAY 7 God, thank you for carrying me through another week. I may not understand your plan, but I can see your mercy in the strength that keeps me standing. Keep teaching me that your goodness doesn't always change my story; it carries me through it, one breath at a time. Amen.

The Shock of Loss

When I can't believe this is my life now

So after you have suffered a little while, he will restore, support, and strengthen you, and he will place you on a firm foundation.

—1 PETER 5:10

Shock is the body and soul's first reaction to loss. It's that blur of disbelief when your mind still reaches for what should be here; when you keep reaching for a future that's suddenly gone. Nothing feels real, and faith can feel just as distant. You move through rooms like a stranger in your own life, functioning on instinct while everything inside you feels frozen.

Peter wrote these words to believers who were suffering, reminding them that pain was not a sign of God's absence. He didn't say suffering wouldn't come; he said it wouldn't last forever. "After you have suffered a little while, he will restore you." Those words don't minimize grief; they acknowledge it and then promise God's patient repair.

In those first weeks after Gracie died, I remember walking through stores on autopilot, stunned that the world kept moving. I couldn't pray or make sense of anything. I wasn't doubting God; I was barely able to think. This verse tells us that God's kindness is still present, even when everything else is numb.

Shock isn't a spiritual problem; it's your whole being trying to survive something it was never supposed to face. That's where God meets you, not demanding belief but simply offering to hold what's too heavy.

Restoration doesn't happen overnight. But in time, he strengthens what's left standing. He places your shaken heart on a firmer foundation—one built not on understanding but on his unchanging love.

DAILY PRAYERS

DAY 1 God, everything still feels unreal. My mind can't keep up with what's happened. Please meet me in this shock. Steady my shaking heart and help me breathe again. Remind me that you are here—even when nothing makes sense—and that I don't have to face this alone. Amen.

DAY 2 Lord, my body feels heavy and my thoughts are scattered. I can't plan, pray, or process. Please cover me with your peace and give my mind rest. Let your presence be the ground beneath my feet when everything else feels like sand. Hold me steady today. Amen.

DAY 3 Father, people say time will heal, but right now time just hurts. I need your strength to get through the minutes. When I feel like I'm falling apart, remind me that you never lose your grip on me. Be my stability when everything else has crumbled. Amen.

DAY 4 God, I don't recognize this version of myself. I feel broken and unfamiliar. Please show me that you still see the person I was and the one you will rebuild. Help me trust that restoration will come, even if I can't imagine what that looks like right now. Amen.

DAY 5 Lord, thank you that your kindness doesn't depend on how strong I am. When shock makes me numb, speak softly to my spirit. Let your comfort seep into the cracks of my heart and remind me that you are still working, even in the silence. Amen.

DAY 6 Father, the days blur together and I feel like I'm just surviving. Help me rest in your promise that this suffering will not last forever. When I can't see past today, hold my eyes on your steady love that never fails. Amen.

DAY 7 God, thank you for staying with me through another week. I'm still broken, but I'm also still breathing. That's grace. Keep restoring what I can't rebuild on my own. Strengthen what remains in me and plant my feet on the firm foundation of your love. Amen.

WEEK 3

When I'm Angry at God

What do I do with the anger that comes after loss?

O my people, trust in him at all times.
Pour out your heart to him,
for God is our refuge.

—Psalm 62:8

Anger after loss isn't gentle. It doesn't show up politely. Sometimes it explodes. Sometimes it gets buried so deep you convince yourself you're fine—until it comes roaring out at the worst possible moment. If you've ever felt so angry you didn't know where to put it, so full of rage and hurt it felt like it was running through every vein in your body, you're not alone.

Psalm 62:8 tells us to "pour out your heart" to God. Not to edit it but to pour it out. That includes anger. David wasn't offering a calm, measured prayer. He was giving us permission to bring everything—rage, confusion, heartbreak—to a God who can hold it.

After Gracie died, I wasn't calm or composed. I cursed God in my angriest moments. I asked why he didn't save her. I believed he could—but he didn't. I tend to bottle emotions, especially anger, until it builds up so much pressure that it explodes. When it came, it came fast and hard.

Here's what I've learned: Anger is a secondary emotion. You're not angry because you're cruel or faithless. You're angry because you're hurt. Because something sacred was taken.

God knows that. He isn't shocked by your anger or offended by your honesty. He shares your grief. He stays when the words get ugly. Letting anger out—

crying, yelling, even screaming—can be a release, not a failure. If you let it stay trapped inside, it can poison you.

If you're angry at God, you're not bad, you're grieving. And the God who tells you to pour out your heart is strong enough to stay while you do.

DAILY PRAYERS

DAY 1 God, I'm furious. I don't know how else to say it. Why didn't you save my child? I believed you could. I begged. This hurts in ways I can't explain. Please don't turn away from me now. Stay here while I say the things I don't know how to soften. Amen.

DAY 2 Lord, this anger keeps rising up no matter how hard I try to contain it. It scares me sometimes. I don't want it to swallow me whole. Help me release it instead of burying it. Can you handle how loud this pain feels inside my body today? Amen.

DAY 3 God, I feel betrayed. I trusted you, and my child still died. I don't know how to reconcile that. Was I wrong to hope? Wrong to believe? I need you to hear me without correcting me. Sit with me in this rage and heartbreak. Don't leave when I'm this honest. Amen.

DAY 4 Father, the anger comes in waves, and I can't always control when it hits. I yell. I cry. I fall apart. Please remind me that this doesn't make me an angry person or faithless. It makes me a mother who lost her child and is hurting deeply. Amen.

DAY 5 God, I'm so tired of holding this in. It feels like my body is full of something that needs to get out. Will you help me release this anger safely? Show me where I can let it go without shame. Meet me in the mess instead of expecting calm. Amen.

DAY 6 Lord, I don't want my anger to turn into bitterness, but I don't want to pretend it isn't here, either. Teach me how to bring it to you honestly. Remind me that you already know what I'm feeling. Can you hold this without asking me to clean it up first? Amen.

DAY 7 God, this week has been heavy with emotions and questions that still don't have answers. Thank you for staying when I've been loud, confused, and angry. Help me trust that you can handle my grief exactly as it is. I'm still here. Please stay with me. Amen.

The Silence After Goodbye

When God feels absent in the quiet after loss

O Lord, how long will you forget me? Forever?
How long will you look the other way?
How long must I struggle with anguish in my
soul, with sorrow in my heart every day?

—Psalm 13:1–2

After the funeral, after the messages stop, the world goes on and silence takes its place. The house is still. The phone doesn't ring. You wake up to the same ache day after day and wonder if God has gone quiet, too. The noise of crisis fades, and what remains is a long stretch of ordinary silence.

That's exactly where David was when he wrote Psalm 13. He wasn't hiding his feelings behind nice words; he was crying out in the emptiness. "O Lord, how long will you forget me? Forever?" These aren't faithless words; they're the language of someone still turning toward God even when it seems like he's far away. David didn't stop talking to God because he felt forgotten. He brought the feeling with him.

Silence doesn't always mean absence. Sometimes it's what remains when words are too small for what's happened. After my own loss, the quiet felt suffocating. I kept waiting for something dramatic—a sign, a clear answer, a sudden sense of relief. Instead, what I received was steadier than that. Not loud. Not obvious. Just a quiet sense that I was not alone in the room.

If you're in the quiet right now, know this: You haven't been abandoned. The God who stood by in your heartbreak is still beside you in the silence. He may not speak with explanations, but his nearness shows up in small ways like a deep breath, a memory, or a sunrise you didn't expect to notice. He is still here.

DAILY PRAYERS

DAY 1 God, this silence is deafening. I keep waiting to feel you, to hear something, anything. Please meet me in the quiet and remind me that even when you don't speak, you're still here, holding me in ways I can't yet see or understand. Amen.

DAY 2 Lord, it feels like everyone else has moved on while I'm still stuck in this ache. When I feel forgotten, whisper to my heart that you still see me. Let your presence be louder than the loneliness. Will you stay close to me when the world goes quiet? Amen.

DAY 3 Lord, when I can't feel you, help me trust that you're still near. My heart is weary, and hope feels thin and fragile. Please remind me that faith isn't about feelings; it's about knowing you're still holding me, even when everything around me has gone quiet. Amen.

DAY 4 Lord, I miss the sound of laughter, the rhythm of what life used to be. This silence feels endless. Please speak to me through small things like a gentle wind, a song, a moment of calm, and remind me that your voice still lives here. Amen.

DAY 5 Father, waiting for you feels hard. I want answers, but all I hear is quiet. Teach me to rest instead of wanting to resist. Let the stillness become sacred. Let it be a place where I can meet you without needing words. Hold my heart steady in the waiting. Amen.

DAY 6 God, this quiet makes me feel unsure. I keep wondering if I'm doing something wrong or if I've somehow drifted too far for you to reach me. Will you remind me that your silence isn't rejection? Please help me feel your nearness in ways my hurting heart can recognize today. Amen.

DAY 7 Father, thank you for staying with me through another week of quiet. The silence still feels heavy sometimes, but I'm beginning to see that you're here even when nothing shifts or sounds different. As I step into a new week, help me trust your steady presence in the places that feel the most quiet. Amen.

WEEK 5

God Wept, Too

When I need to know that God understands my pain

Then Jesus wept. The people who were standing nearby said, "See how much he loved him!"

—JOHN 11:35–36

Lazarus wasn't just anyone to Jesus; he was his friend. Scripture tells us that Jesus loved Lazarus and his sisters, Mary and Martha, deeply. So when word came that Lazarus was sick and later that he'd died, Jesus didn't respond like a distant Savior; he responded like someone whose heart had broken, too.

When Jesus arrived, both sisters said what grieving hearts often do: "Lord, if you had been here, this wouldn't have happened." And then comes the shortest verse in the Bible, and maybe the most revealing: "Jesus wept."

He didn't correct them. He didn't quote Scripture or offer explanations. He stood beside them and cried. He already knew the comfort the resurrection would bring, but he still entered the pain of the moment. That's the kind of God we have. A God who feels with us before he fixes anything around us.

If you've ever wondered whether God truly understands your heartbreak, this story is your answer. He does. He's felt loss. He's stood at graves. He's watched people he loves grieve and it moved him to tears.

Jesus doesn't rush your sorrow or demand you to be strong. He sits in it with you. His tears are proof that your pain is not unseen, and his presence is proof that love still lives here.

DAILY PRAYERS

DAY 1 Jesus, you know how it feels to stand at a grave. You don't hide from the pain; you enter it. Please enter mine, too. Sit with me in this grief and remind me that my tears are safe with you. They matter to the God who wept. Amen.

DAY 2 Lord, when others don't understand or they try to rush me forward, remind me that you never hurry grief. You paused to weep with those you loved. Help me rest in that truth and believe that my sorrow is honored by you. Amen.

DAY 3 Father, it comforts me to know that you understand pain. When loss feels too heavy to bear, remind me that you carried it first. Help me find peace in your empathy and strength in your presence, knowing you never ask me to face this alone. Amen.

DAY 4 God, sometimes I feel guilty that I'm still crying. Remind me that even you cried. Show me that tears aren't weakness. They're love that's still alive. Help me feel your nearness in every wave of emotion and teach me to grieve without shame. Amen.

DAY 5 Lord, thank you for being a God who feels. You didn't skip over pain to prove power; you showed compassion first. Help me reflect that same compassion toward myself and others. Let empathy, not fear, guide how I move through my grief. Amen.

DAY 6 Jesus, when I think of your tears at Lazarus's tomb, I'm reminded that you see all that's broken in the world. Please hold what feels shattered in me. Let your gentleness steady my heart and remind me that my sorrow is never wasted with you. Amen.

DAY 7 God, thank you for understanding what it feels like to lose and to love deeply. As I face another week, let the truth of your compassion stay close. You're not distant from my pain; you're present in it, and that changes everything. Amen.

WEEK 6

Why Did This Happen?

Bringing my hardest questions to a God who can handle them

"I am disgusted with my life.
Let me complain freely.
My bitter soul must complain.
I will say to God, 'Don't simply condemn me—
tell me the charge you are bringing against me.' "

—Job 10:1–2

Job knew how it felt to lose everything. His children were gone, his body was covered in pain, and the God he had always trusted suddenly felt distant. In this passage, he doesn't hold anything back. He says exactly what's in his heart: raw, unfiltered, and real.

That's what grief does. It strips away the polite versions of our faith and leaves us face to face with our questions. *Why did this happen? Why my child? Why didn't you stop it?* If you've ever whispered those words, you're in good company.

Job's honesty didn't disqualify him from God's love; it drew God near. At the end of the story, God doesn't rebuke Job for his words; he honors his honesty. Job never got the answers he wanted, and on this side of heaven, neither will we. But he did encounter something steadier than an explanation: He encountered God himself.

Here's why that matters: An answer might have satisfied Job's mind for a moment, but it would not have held him through the rest of his life. What held him was the realization that God had not abandoned him.

Knowing God more deeply didn't erase his loss. It didn't justify it. But it anchored him in a way an explanation never could.

You don't need to edit your pain before you bring it to him. He already knows your thoughts. Let him meet you in your "why." The same God who didn't walk away from Job won't walk away from you, either. He can handle your heartbreak, and he loves you right in the middle of it.

DAILY PRAYERS

DAY 1 God, I don't understand any of this. Everything in me wants to know why this happened. Why my child? Why this way? Please hold me in the questions that have no answers. Help me trust that you're still here even when understanding feels impossible. Amen.

DAY 2 Lord, the questions come in waves, and I don't have the strength to fight them off anymore. I'm tired of trying to make sense of what I'll never fully understand. Please calm the storm inside me and stay close in the places that feel unclear. Hold me through the unknown. Amen.

DAY 3 Father, I've asked you why more times than I can count and you've stayed silent. That silence hurts, but I'm trying to believe you haven't gone anywhere. Please meet me in the ache of not knowing and hold me steady while my heart wrestles for peace. Amen.

DAY 4 God, it's hard not to feel forgotten. So many things in life make no sense anymore. When I start to doubt your goodness, remind me of who you are. Show me glimpses of your love, even in small ways, and help me keep talking to you through all the confusion. Amen.

DAY 5 Lord, I'm realizing that some questions won't be answered on this side of heaven, and that's hard to accept. Please help me live with that tension. To hold space for both confusion and faith. Teach me to find comfort in your presence, even without understanding your plan. Amen.

DAY 6 Father, when I can't make sense of your ways, let me fall back on your character. You are still kind, you are still faithful, and you are still love. Help me remember that truth when everything else feels uncertain. I don't have all the answers, but I still have you. Amen.

DAY 7 God, I know there are mysteries about this life that I'll never understand, and losing my child is the hardest of them all. Will you hold me in the questions I can't untangle? As I step into a new week, help me trust that even in the midst of what I can't explain, you are still with me. Amen.

My Body Feels the Grief, Too

When loss hurts everywhere—mind, body, and soul

Have mercy on me, LORD, for I am in distress.
Tears blur my eyes.
My body and soul are withering away.
I am dying from grief;
my years are shortened by sadness.
Sin has drained my strength;
I am wasting away from within.

—PSALM 31:9–10

This passage puts words to what your body already knows: Grief doesn't just live in your heart. It hurts everywhere. It clouds your vision, weakens your body, and makes each breath feel heavier than the last. The psalmist's cry is raw and real: "I am dying from grief."

If you've felt that, too, you're not dramatic or weak. The physical side of loss is real. The exhaustion, the tight chest, the sleepless nights, the brain fog that makes simple tasks feel impossible—they're all part of deep sorrow. Trauma settles into muscle and bone. Your body carries what your heart cannot process all at once.

When Gracie died, I couldn't eat for months. There was a sharp ache in my chest that reached up into my throat. I thought something was physically wrong with me. In many ways, something was. My body was grieving. It felt like it was breaking right alongside my heart.

But slowly—so slowly—relief began to come. The pain didn't disappear, but it softened. My appetite came back. My breath came easier. That's how God works in grief. He doesn't demand that you be strong; he offers his strength to steady you.

Your body will not always feel like this. The sharp pain will dull and the heaviness will lift in small ways. It's not a sign that you're "moving on"; it's proof that you're still being held. God is gently restoring what heartbreak has worn down, until rest feels possible again.

DAILY PRAYERS

DAY 1 Lord, my body feels heavy with sorrow. I wake up tired, and simple things take all my strength. Please hold me when I can't hold myself up. Help me feel your rest in my bones and remind me that I'm still held, even when I'm completely worn out. Amen.

DAY 2 God, the nights are the hardest. My mind races and my body refuses to rest. When sleep feels impossible, will you calm my thoughts and quiet my heart? Cover me in peace that doesn't depend on understanding. Let me drift into rest knowing you are near. Amen.

DAY 3 Father, my heart aches in ways words can't explain. Grief has settled in my chest like a weight I can't get off. Please loosen what feels bound up inside me. Let every breath remind me that I am still alive, still loved, and still yours. Amen.

DAY 4 Lord, I've lost my appetite for so much: food, joy, life itself. Will you take away this lump in my throat and ease the pain? Please nourish me in small ways today. Let your presence become my sustenance until I can eat, laugh, and live again without guilt. Amen.

DAY 5 God, I feel anxious and tense, like my whole body is bracing for something that's already happened. Please teach my muscles to unclench and my spirit to rest. Remind me that I don't have to carry this alone and that you are strong enough for both of us. Amen.

DAY 6 Father, today I want to move again. To walk, to breathe, to feel the air fill my lungs. Please give me the strength to start small. Meet me in motion, even if all I can manage is a single step. Let healing begin there. Amen.

DAY 7 Lord, my body has carried so much pain and yet here I am still breathing. Thank you for holding me through every sleepless night and weary morning. Continue to restore what grief has taken. Let peace settle into my bones and remind me that you're not finished with me yet. Amen.

WEEK 8

What to Do with Guilt

When I keep on replaying the what-ifs

Our actions will show that we belong to the truth, so we will be confident when we stand before God. Even if we feel guilty, God is greater than our feelings, and he knows everything.

—1 JOHN 3:19–20

Guilt after loss feels endless. Your mind replays every detail, searching for the one moment that could have changed everything. *What if I'd noticed sooner? What if I'd made a different choice? What if I had done something more?* The questions circle like they're looking for a verdict and somehow you're always the one on trial.

I've asked those same questions. I blamed myself for things I can't stop replaying in my mind. A piña colada I drank before I knew I was pregnant, medicine my doctor said was safe but wasn't, the very last night I left her hospital room when something inside told me to stay. The what-ifs never stop whispering, *Maybe it's your fault.* Guilt can feel like the only way to stay connected, as if punishing yourself proves how much you loved them.

But here's what's true: If love could have saved your child, they would still be here. You did everything a mother could do with what you knew at the time. You made decisions out of love, not neglect. You carried, nurtured, and cared for them as best you could, and that was enough.

1 John 3:19–20 reminds us that even when guilt screams louder than reason, God knows the full story. He saw your heart in every moment. He knows your motives, your love, your exhaustion, and your ache. And he does not blame you. The one who knows *everything* says you are not at fault. Not now, not ever.

DAILY PRAYERS

DAY 1 God, my mind won't stop replaying every moment. I keep searching for what I missed, what I could've done differently. Please quiet the noise of guilt. Help me believe that you saw it all and that nothing I did or didn't do could have changed the outcome you already knew. Amen.

DAY 2 Lord, I feel like I failed my child. My heart keeps accusing me, but you said you're greater than my feelings. Remind me that you know everything, including the things I understood and the things I couldn't have known. Let your truth speak louder than my shame. Amen.

DAY 3 Father, the what-ifs haunt me. What if I had known sooner, done more, seen a sign I missed? You know how much I wanted to protect them. Please lift the weight of guilt I was never meant to carry and fill the empty places with your peace. Amen.

DAY 4 God, I keep thinking love should have been enough to save them. But I know you're reminding me that love was never the problem. I loved them fiercely. Thank you for seeing my heart, not my missteps. Help me rest in the truth that love was always enough. Amen.

DAY 5 Lord, I believed lies that said this was my fault. Today, I want to release them back to you. Show me the difference between guilt that destroys and conviction that heals. Help me walk in freedom knowing you never blame me for what I can't control. Amen.

DAY 6 God, you know every detail, every decision, every fear, and every tear I've cried since that day. You've seen my sleepless nights and my desperate prayers. Help me accept your grace. Let your voice be louder than the guilt that tries to steal my peace. Amen.

DAY 7 Father, I may never stop wishing the story ended differently, but I'm learning to trust that you see what I can't. Thank you for holding both my child and me in your mercy. When guilt tries to return, remind me again: I did the best I could. Amen.

When People Say the Wrong Thing

Words that miss the mark

Singing cheerful songs to a person with a heavy heart
is like taking someone's coat in cold weather
or pouring vinegar in a wound.

—Proverbs 25:20

When your heart is broken, even kind words can sting. Someone says, "They're in a better place," "At least you have other kids," or "Everything happens for a reason." They mean well, but their words land like vinegar on an open wound.

Proverbs 25:20 shows us that God understands this dynamic. He doesn't call your sensitivity "weakness." He knows that when your soul is raw, misplaced cheerfulness hurts. It's like standing shivering in the cold while someone takes your coat and says, "Be grateful you had one," which is similar to saying, "You're young, you can have more." It's not cruel on purpose, but it misses the reality of your pain.

After Gracie died, I heard all those phrases. People were using words to try to make sense of the unthinkable. What I needed wasn't answers, though; I needed presence. Someone to sit in the silence, to say her name, to weep with me. That's the kind of comfort Jesus gives. He doesn't minimize pain; he meets us in it.

Jesus never responds to suffering with slogans. He responds with presence. He weeps. He touches. He stays. And that's what we want from people, too, right?

If careless words have wounded you, know this: God's voice never sounds like that. He doesn't rush your grief or explain it away. He stays with you in the cold and offers his own coat instead. The next time someone's words sting, remember that they're coming from a place of discomfort. Let God's compassion speak louder.

DAILY PRAYERS

DAY 1 Lord, some words still echo in my head, and they hurt more than anyone realizes. Please remind me that you never speak to me that way. When other people's words sting, let yours be louder, softer, and truer. Help me feel the difference between their discomfort and your compassion. Amen.

DAY 2 God, I know people mean well but their words sometimes make the ache worse. When they say things that minimize my pain, give me patience to respond with grace and wisdom to set boundaries. Teach me to rest in your understanding when no one else seems to get it. Amen.

DAY 3 Father, when people's words feel dismissive, it cuts deep. I know they mean well, but it hurts when my pain is brushed aside. Please meet me in that loneliness. Remind me that you never dismiss my grief and that my sorrow is safe with you. Amen.

DAY 4 Lord, sometimes I want to shout, "Please stop talking!" I am tired of pretending other people's words don't hurt. Give me courage to be honest about my pain and peace to forgive their ignorance. Help me remember that even when they fail me, you never do. Amen.

DAY 5 God, you see how often I bite my tongue, how many times I smile to keep the peace. Please help me release the anger I feel when others speak carelessly. Teach me to hand that frustration back to you instead of letting it harden my heart. Amen.

DAY 6 Father, I am grateful for the few who listen instead of just talking, who sit beside me without trying to fix anything. Bless those who choose silence and presence over empty answers. Help me be that kind of comfort to others who grieve, too. Amen.

DAY 7 Lord, today I want to pray for the people who don't know what to say. I know most of them mean well, but they don't understand this kind of pain. Soften their hearts, teach them compassion, and help me forgive in those times when words have wounded me. Let your grace cover us both. Amen.

WEEK 10

The Loneliness of Grief

When people disappear and silence becomes your new normal

I look for someone to come and help me,
but no one gives me a passing thought!
No one will help me;
no one cares a bit what happens to me.
Then I pray to you, O LORD.
I say, "You are my place of refuge."

—PSALM 142:4–5

There is a kind of loneliness that words can't fix: the ache of empty arms. The space where they should be. It's a kind of silence that hums through every ordinary moment, reminding you that someone is missing.

After Gracie passed away, a lot of friends and family disappeared, too. When I did see them, they avoided eye contact and talking to me one-on-one, like I had a contagious disease or something. I didn't get casseroles dropped off like in the movies. When someone finally did speak to me, they tiptoed on eggshells around me, afraid I might crack if they said her name.

It's human nature to avoid what feels uncomfortable. People don't mean to hurt us; they simply don't know what to say. Grief reminds them of their own fragility, their own fears about loss, so instead of drawing near, they pull away.

David knew that kind of loneliness. In Psalm 142, he is hiding in a cave, completely abandoned and unseen. He says, "No one gives me a passing thought." But then he turns to God and says, "You are my place of refuge."

That moment matters. David's circumstances did not change, but his focus did. He discovered that even in isolation, God stayed close. God doesn't always remove us from the lonely place, but instead, he fills it with his presence.

You don't have your child in your arms right now, and yet, you are not alone in that emptiness. The God who wept over death is the one who sits beside you in it. He does not avoid your grief; he shares it.

DAILY PRAYERS

DAY 1 God, this loneliness feels endless. My arms ache for what should be here, for the weight and warmth of the child I long to hold. Please fill the emptiness with your presence. Let your nearness be as real as the ache itself and remind me that I am never truly alone. Amen.

DAY 2 Lord, people have drifted away, and I don't know how to reach for them anymore. The phone stays quiet, and the days feel long. Please meet me here in this loneliness. Surround me with your comfort until I can feel your presence steadying me again. Amen.

DAY 3 Father, sometimes I wish someone would just say my child's name out loud. The silence feels heavier than the grief itself. Please remind me that you never stop speaking their name. You remember them perfectly and you hold every part of their story close to your heart. Amen.

DAY 4 God, help me forgive the ones who disappeared. I know they were scared or unsure of what to say. Give them courage to come closer and the grace to listen without fixing. Let them see that presence means more than answers. Bless them for trying, even if they stumble. Amen.

DAY 5 Lord, there are moments when I wonder if anyone sees how much this hurts. The loneliness feels louder than any noise. Whisper to my heart that you see it all, even what I never say out loud. Be my steady companion in the spaces where people cannot reach. Amen.

DAY 6 Father, I miss community—the laughter and the warmth of being known. Please bring safe people back into my life; the ones who can handle my tears without turning away. Teach me to receive love again, even when it feels risky. Help me believe connection is still possible. Amen.

DAY 7 God, I wish things were different. I wish this house was filled with laughter again. But since it's not, would you fill my heart with your peace? Meet me in the quiet and remind me that you're not afraid of it. You're here, even in the silence. Amen.

It Feels Like I'm Being Punished

Was it something I did?

"Rabbi," his disciples asked him, "why was this man born blind? Was it because of his own sins or his parents' sins?"
"It was not because of his sins or his parents' sins," Jesus answered. "This happened so the power of God could be seen in him."

—JOHN 9:2–3

After loss, guilt starts whispering lies like, *Maybe God is punishing me. Maybe I did something wrong. Maybe this happened because of me.* Those thoughts aren't random; they're the heart's desperate attempt to make sense of something that will never make sense.

The disciples asked Jesus a question just like that. As they walked with him, they saw a man blind from birth and wanted to know whose fault it was that he was blind. "Was it because of his own sins or his parents' sins?" It was an honest question, born from the same pain that asks, *Why me? Why my child?*

Jesus didn't respond with blame or theories—he answered with compassion and truth. "It was not because of his sins or his parents' sins." Instead of assigning fault or explaining further, he acted. He bent down, mixed mud with his hands, placed it on the man's eyes, and gave him sight.

I've asked the same question you may be asking now: *If he can heal, why didn't he heal my child?* Scripture tells us this world is still broken, still waiting for full redemption. Your child's healing didn't happen here on earth, but they now live restored with him in a place where nothing broken remains. And God stays with you in the gap between here and heaven.

This is not your punishment. God didn't take your child to teach you a lesson or pay you back for anything in your past. You didn't cause this. You didn't fail. God's heart breaks with yours, and he is still good.

DAILY PRAYERS

DAY 1 God, I keep wondering if this happened because of something I did. The guilt feels heavy and I can't shake the thought that you might be angry with me. Please remind me of what is true. You don't punish me through pain; you love me through it. Amen.

DAY 2 Lord, the question "Why me?" never leaves my mind. I know you see my heart and how much I loved my child. Please quiet the lies that say this is my fault. Remind me that you are kind and that your love never works through punishment. Amen.

DAY 3 Father, I still replay every decision, every moment, wondering if I could have changed the outcome. I know you saw it all, every heartbeat and tear. Help me trust that you are not a God of payback, but a God of mercy. Teach me to rest in that truth. Amen.

DAY 4 God, sometimes I picture you watching from far away, deciding what happens and what does not. But I know that is not who you are. You are near, grieving with me, holding me through this pain. Help me remember that your heart breaks alongside mine. Amen.

DAY 5 Lord, the thought that you could be punishing me is too much to carry. Please lift that lie off my shoulders. Replace it with the truth that you sent Jesus to take my punishment once and for all. You are not angry with me; you are for me. Amen.

DAY 6 Father, I don't understand why this happened, but I want to believe that your love is still here. When I cannot see it, show me small reminders of your kindness. Teach me that sorrow is not your wrath, and grief is not your rejection. Hold me close tonight. Amen.

DAY 7 God, thank you for seeing the truth of my heart even when guilt clouds it. Thank you that nothing I've done could make you love me less. Help me rest in your mercy and remember that you are not punishing me. You are here to heal what this world has broken. Amen.

WEEK 12

When I'm Too Tired to Pray

Resting in a wordless prayer

And the Holy Spirit helps us in
our weakness. For example, we don't know what
God wants us to pray for. But the Holy Spirit
prays for us with groanings that
cannot be expressed in words.

—ROMANS 8:26

There may be days when you sit in the same spot for hours, staring at the floor, and all you can manage is a sigh. Grief steals your energy, your focus, sometimes even your faith. You want to talk to God, but you're too tired to start, and the guilt for not praying only adds another layer of pain.

Romans 8:26 speaks directly into that exhaustion. It tells us that the Holy Spirit helps us in our weakness. That means when you don't have words, when your mind feels foggy, when even forming a sentence feels impossible, you are not failing at prayer. God already knows what's in your heart. When you cannot pray, the Spirit prays for you. He gathers every tear, every groan, every shaky breath, and carries them to the Father as a prayer on your behalf.

So what does prayer look like when you have no words left? It might mean folding your hands when you're lying in bed, too tired to move. Maybe it's kneeling beside the bed, crying, sighing, or just thinking of God. Maybe you whisper in your mind what you need right now: peace, rest, courage to face the day, or a dream where you see your child's face again. Maybe you just want him to send someone to say their name out loud.

All of that counts as prayer. God doesn't need your polish; he just wants your presence. Even your silence speaks when your heart turns toward him.

DAILY PRAYERS

DAY 1 Holy Spirit, I don't have words today. My mind is foggy and my body is tired. I can't pray like I want to, but I still want to feel close to you. Please meet me here in the quiet and hear the parts of me that don't know how to speak. Amen.

DAY 2 Lord, thank you for understanding what I can't say. Thank you that you don't need me to sound polished. When my prayers come out as tears or silence, please receive them as they are and remind me that you're still listening, even when I'm quiet. Amen.

DAY 3 Father, I'm learning that you hear me even when all I do is sit and breathe. That gives me comfort. Help me stop feeling guilty for not having the right words. Teach me that you care more about my honesty than my eloquence. Meet me here. Amen.

DAY 4 God, tonight I don't even know what to ask for. My heart feels heavy, and I'm worn thin. Please remind me that you understand sighs and tears just as much as words. Let your peace wrap around me like a blanket and let rest become my prayer's answer tonight. Amen.

DAY 5 Lord, sometimes I feel like my silence makes me distant from you, but I know that isn't true. You never leave, and you never grow tired of me. Thank you for staying close even when I have nothing left to say. God, help me feel you when I can't pray. Amen.

DAY 6 Lord, you know how tired I am. Thank you for being patient with me. I don't have strength for long prayers, but I know you still listen. Let your presence fill the quiet spaces and remind me that being with you, even in silence, is enough. Amen.

DAY 7 God, thank you for seeing my limits and knowing how much this hurts. Thank you for meeting me in my weariness and turning even my quiet times into prayer. When I can't reach for you, remind me that you're already holding me. Amen.

The Ache of What Should Have Been

When seeing others with children stirs a pain I can't explain

[W]hile my enemies continually taunt me, saying,
"Where is this God of yours?"
My heart is breaking
as I remember how it used to be . . .
Why am I discouraged?
Why is my heart so sad?
I will put my hope in God!
I will praise him again . . .

—PSALM 42:3–5

There's something about seeing other people's joy that makes your loss ache all over again. It happens quietly, like a stroller in a store aisle, a family photo, a baby giggling in church. No one else notices the way your chest tightens, but God does.

This psalm says, "My heart is breaking as I remember how it used to be." That's what this feels like: remembering the life that once was, the milestones that should be happening now, the birthdays you'll never get to plan.

When Gracie died, I couldn't hold another baby for years. People would ask if I wanted to, thinking it might bring comfort, but it didn't. I'd say, "No, thank you," and go home feeling like I'd failed some invisible test. But God never saw my "no" as failure. He saw a heart doing its best to survive.

Grief isn't jealousy; it's love with nowhere to land. And that ache you feel when you see someone else's joy? God understands it completely. He isn't ashamed of you for feeling it. He meets you right there, hand over your heart, whispering, *I see you. I know. I'm still here.*

Even when the sight of another child stops you in your tracks, God hasn't turned from you. He's walking with you through every reminder, holding what still hurts, and staying close in the places you'd rather avoid. He won't rush you past it. He'll sit with you in it.

DAILY PRAYERS

DAY 1 God, some days my heart aches without warning. It's the small things that bring the sting back. I don't want to hide from it, but I also don't know how to live with it. Please meet me in these moments when missing my child feels too heavy to name. Amen.

DAY 2 Lord, I see joy around me and sometimes it hurts. I wish I could join in, but the ache gets in the way. Please remind me that you understand why it's hard. Help me release the guilt for feeling both love and pain at the same time. Amen.

DAY 3 Father, I feel caught between two worlds. The one where I love my child deeply and the one where the world expects me to move on. Please give me grace for myself when I can't. Help me remember you're not impatient with my grief. You're sitting in it with me. Amen.

DAY 4 God, I still have limits I wish I didn't. Some places and conversations press on grief that still feels tender and exposed. Remind me that setting boundaries isn't a lack of faith; it's how I take care of my heart. Thank you for understanding my quiet and my "no." Amen.

DAY 5 Lord, I don't know when this ache will soften. I want to hope for that day but right now it still hurts to imagine. Please hold what I can't fix and let me feel your compassion instead of shame. Teach me to rest in the truth that you see it all. Amen.

DAY 6 Father, when I think of what could have been, it feels like a whole life missing from the world. Please help me remember my child's story isn't lost to you. You hold what I can't hold anymore, and you still see the love that hasn't found its place. Amen.

DAY 7 God, some days I can watch the world move around me and feel peace. Other days it hurts to see that someone else gets to hold their baby while I cannot. Please hold that ache for me. Teach me to rest in your love, even when the unfairness feels impossible to bear. Amen.

PART 2

When Faith Feels Fragile: Wrestling Honestly with God

WEEK 14

When I Miss Who I Used to Be

Learning to live with the version of myself that grief created

This means that anyone who belongs to Christ has become a new person. The old life is gone; a new life has begun!

—2 CORINTHIANS 5:17

There was a version of you that existed before your child died, and maybe you miss her so much it catches you off guard. She felt lighter, happier. She didn't scan every room for reminders of what she's lost. She didn't wake up already tired from carrying a pain that never fully lets go.

When Paul talks about becoming a "new person" in Christ, he's talking about salvation, not grief; but the truth is, loss changes you, too. It reshapes what you can handle, how you think, how deeply things hit you, and even how you show up in the world. You didn't choose this "new you"—she just arrived one day after everything fell apart.

And here's the thing: You didn't become this person because your faith wasn't strong enough. You became her because your heart absorbed a blow no parent should ever experience. Anyone would be changed by that.

There's also this pressure people put on grieving moms. The pressure to "bounce back" or to be the comeback story. As if healing is something you can perform on a stage. It's not, and you can ask God to take that pressure off you. You don't owe anyone a recovery arc.

God isn't waiting for you to go back to who you were before. He's forming a new you—not a "better" version, just a truer one: the woman doing her best to breathe, to love, to keep going. And he stays with you as you learn how to live inside this unfamiliar life.

DAILY PRAYERS

DAY 1 God, I miss who I was before loss changed me. I don't always like the version of myself I live with now: the heaviness, the edge, the exhaustion. Please meet me in this place I never wanted to be. Help me trust that you still see someone worth holding and helping. Amen.

DAY 2 Lord, grief has changed the way I move through the world, and I'm trying to understand who I am now. Please give me patience with myself. Remind me that you aren't asking me to be who I used to be. Walk with me as I learn how to exist again. Amen.

DAY 3 Father, my faith feels different than it did before loss. Sometimes smaller, sometimes softer, sometimes unsure. Please hold me in the places that feel unsteady. Help me trust that you aren't disappointed in my questions or shaken confidence. Stay close as I figure out what faith looks like now. Amen.

DAY 4 God, I feel so much pressure to be the comeback story everyone expects. But I'm tired. I can't perform healing. Will you take that weight off me? Help me ask, "What do *you* want for me, God?" instead of "Who do they need me to be?" Amen.

DAY 5 Lord, some days I feel strong, and other days I feel like I'm starting over. Please steady me and help me believe that growth doesn't mean forgetting and change doesn't mean failure. Stay near as I navigate this version of myself that I never asked for but am trying to understand. Amen.

DAY 6 Father, when I feel overwhelmed by how much I've changed, remind me that you saw this version of me long before I did. Help me trust that nothing about me is hidden from you. Fill the parts of me that feel empty with your quiet and steady presence. Amen.

DAY 7 God, thank you for staying with me through every version of myself, even the new version I struggle to accept. Teach me to be gentle with my own heart, and help me believe that who I am becoming matters to you and you're shaping me with patience and love. Amen.

Faith and Doubt Can Coexist

When believing feels hard after loss

"... Have mercy on us and help us, if you can."
"What do you mean, 'If I can'?" Jesus asked.
"Anything is possible if a person believes."
The father instantly cried out,
"I do believe, but help me overcome my unbelief!"

—MARK 9:22–24

Grief has a way of shaking what you believe. Not destroying it—just shaking it. You may still trust God, but not in the same way. You may believe but also feel unsure. That mix of faith and uncertainty doesn't make you broken—it makes you human.

The father in Mark 9 understood that kind of faith. His son had suffered for years and nothing helped. By the time he reached Jesus, he wasn't confident or full of hope—he was worn out. Unsure if Jesus could help. Unsure if asking would even matter. His words were honest: "Help us, if you can," which is really another way of saying, "I want to trust, but I don't know if I can."

Jesus didn't correct him or ask for stronger faith; he invited honesty, and the father answered with one of the truest prayers in Scripture: "I do believe, but help me overcome my unbelief." Jesus honored that prayer. He met the father right in the middle of his fear, not on the other side of it.

If part of you believes and part of you doubts, that doesn't mean your faith is failing. It means your world has been shattered and you're trying to make sense of God inside that brokenness. Losing a child changes how you see everything, including him.

God doesn't step back when your faith feels unsteady; he draws close. He meets you in the questions, sits with you in the tension, and holds you through every uneven and fragile step.

DAILY PRAYERS

DAY 1 God, believing feels complicated now. I want to trust you, but losing my child changed everything. Please hold me in this place where my heart feels torn in two. Meet me in the fear, the anger, and the confusion. Show me you are still here, even when I'm unsure of you. Amen.

DAY 2 Lord, I miss the simple faith I used to have. Now everything feels shaky. Please help me stop pretending I'm stronger than I am. Sit with me in the tension between wanting to believe and struggling to understand. Help me remember that you don't leave when my faith feels fragile. Amen.

DAY 3 Father, I never imagined I would struggle to trust you like this. What am I supposed to do with all these questions? Help me be honest without feeling ashamed of my doubt. Remind me that you stay close even when I can't feel it and you hold me when believing feels almost impossible. Amen.

DAY 4 God, sometimes I feel guilty for questioning you, but I don't know how to stop. My mind keeps circling back to the same question: If you are good, why didn't things turn out differently? Please meet me there. Teach me that you can handle every question I bring. Amen.

DAY 5 Lord, I want to feel close to you again, but some days it's hard to sense anything at all. Will you meet me in this quiet place? Help me notice even the smallest reminders that you haven't gone anywhere. Just something simple to steady my heart today. Amen.

DAY 6 Father, my faith feels all over the place. One minute I think I'm okay, and the next I'm falling apart again. I hate feeling this unstable, but you already know that. Will you stay close while I sort through this? I need you to hold what I can't hold anymore. Amen.

DAY 7 God, today I'm choosing honesty over strength. I believe, but I struggle. I hope, but I question. Please take this mixed-up faith and make something of it. Show me that you draw near not because my belief is perfect, but because you are patient and compassionate when I'm hurting. Amen.

WEEK 16

When God Feels Silent

Holding on when waiting for God feels unbearable

Yet I am confident I will see the LORD's goodness
while I am here in the land of the living.
Wait patiently for the LORD.
Be brave and courageous.
Yes, wait patiently for the LORD.

—PSALM 27:13–14

When God feels silent, waiting can feel like a full-time job you never asked for. You pray, you listen, you beg for something to shift . . . and nothing seems to happen. It's especially painful after losing a child, when you already feel abandoned by the life you thought you'd have. Waiting can feel like one more layer on the pile of heartbreak.

Psalm 27 isn't written from a peaceful place. David wrote these words while running for his life, while everything around him was falling apart. He was exhausted and overwhelmed, waiting for God to move and wondering how much longer he could hold on. Still, he said, "I am confident I will see the LORD's goodness," not because he felt it, but because he trusted God would eventually move.

Waiting on God doesn't mean pretending you're okay or feeling peaceful or patient or strong. Sometimes waiting looks like waking up again with a tired soul and saying, "God, I don't see anything changing, but I'm still here."

Waiting is not passive. It's choosing to stay connected to God when he feels quiet. It's choosing to believe he hasn't disappeared, even when you can't feel him. And it's trusting, sometimes just barely, that his goodness is still ahead of you, not behind you.

You don't have to wait perfectly. You just have to keep breathing, keep turning toward him, and keep letting him hold the space you can't fill. He's not ignoring you; he is with you in the quiet, working in ways you can't yet see.

DAILY PRAYERS

DAY 1 God, the quiet feels heavy today. I keep waiting for you to show me something, but nothing seems to shift. Are you still here with me in this silence? Please sit with me while I wait. Help me believe that your stillness doesn't mean you've left. Hold my heart steady tonight. Amen.

DAY 2 Father, waiting feels exhausting. I'm tired of hoping for comfort that hasn't come yet. Will you remind me that you see me waiting even when I can't feel you watching over me? Give me enough strength for just this one moment so the silence doesn't feel like it's swallowing me whole. Amen.

DAY 3 Lord, I don't know what to do with this long pause between prayers and answers. What am I supposed to do while you're quiet? Please help me wait without feeling forgotten. Show me the small ways you are still working, even if I don't recognize them right away. I need that reassurance. Amen.

DAY 4 Father, the silence makes my arms feel even emptier. I wish I could hold my child again, even for a second. Will you carry that longing with me? Remind me that you see the love behind this ache, and that you're not ignoring the places where my heart still breaks. Amen.

DAY 5 Lord, waiting for you feels harder when every memory of my child hurts and comforts at the same time. Will you sit with me in that tension? Help me feel your nearness in the places where their absence feels sharpest. Will you stay close while I wait? Amen.

DAY 6 God, I'm sitting here in this quiet place doing my best to listen. My eyes and ears are fixed on you and I'm paying attention. Please meet me in this moment and let me sense your nearness. My heart is open to whatever you have for me. Amen.

DAY 7 God, another week has gone by, and I still miss my child with every breath. I don't need big answers, but could you give me one small sign that you're here in this? Something gentle I won't miss? Help me trust that your silence isn't distance. Please stay near. Amen.

Why Did God Take Them?

When the question "Why?" has no clear answer

You saw me before I was born.
Every day of my life was recorded in your book.
Every moment was laid out
before a single day had passed.

—PSALM 139:16

"Why did God take my child?" It's a question almost every grieving parent whispers at some point. It's raw, it's honest, and it's the kind of question that rises from deep pain, not rebellion. I've asked it, too. When Gracie died, I wondered if God had decided it was her time or if he reached down and chose to bring her home. That thought made me angry, confused, and terrified.

But Scripture doesn't say he *took* her. It says he *knew* her. He formed her. He wrote her days, not as a puppet master pulling strings but as a Father who knew her story in a world that isn't what he originally designed. We live in a broken world where bodies fail, hearts stop, doctors are human, and tragedies happen that God never called "good."

Psalm 139:16 reminds us that our child's life was not random or forgotten. God did not steal them from us; he received them. He welcomed them into a place where brokenness can't touch them anymore. That's different from taking.

We won't get the full "why" on this side of heaven. That's one of the hardest parts of grief.

But here is the truth Scripture gives us: God did not abandon your child in their last moment, and he has not abandoned you in the aftermath. He is not the cause of your pain, but he is the one who remains in it, steady and close, until the day when he will come again to heal the world.

DAILY PRAYERS

DAY 1 God, I keep asking why my child isn't here anymore. Please hold me in the places that feel confused and angry. Help me trust that you didn't take them from me, but you received them with love. Stay close while I wrestle with questions I can't answer. Amen.

DAY 2 God, I'm struggling to make sense of how a world you created can break this badly. It hurts to know my child's body couldn't stay here. Will you remind me that this brokenness was never your plan? Help me hold on to what is true, even when everything around me feels shattered. Amen.

DAY 3 Father, I don't understand how my child's story fits into this broken world. But I know they were loved, known, and seen by you. Give me comfort in knowing their last breath wasn't the end of their story. Help me believe you are still good, even here. Amen.

DAY 4 God, the thought that you might have taken my child still haunts me. Will you speak truth into that fear? Show me that your heart breaks with mine and that you never call a child's death "good." Stay near as I learn to see you clearly again. Amen.

DAY 5 Lord, some days I blame you without meaning to. You can handle my honesty, but please guide me back to what is true. Teach me that you didn't cause this pain but that you're the one carrying me through it. Help me feel less alone in my questions. Amen.

DAY 6 God, I miss my child so much. The ache makes everything feel complicated, even how I see you. Will you hold my grief gently? Quiet the lies the enemy keeps telling me that say this was my fault or yours. Give me strength to breathe and keep going. Amen.

DAY 7 Father, thank you for being patient with my questions and my broken faith. As I move into another week, will you remind me that you are the author of life? You are the one who restores, receives, and stays. Help me rest in that truth tonight. Amen.

WEEK 18

When God Didn't Answer the Prayer I Begged Hardest For

Facing the heartbreak of prayers that didn't change the outcome

I cry out to God; yes, I shout.
Oh, that God would listen to me!
When I was in deep trouble,
I searched for the Lord.
All night long I prayed, with hands lifted toward
heaven, but my soul was not comforted.

—PSALM 77:1–2

There's a kind of prayer you only pray when your child's life is on the line. The desperate kind, the begging kind. The kind that comes from a place deeper than language. Most mothers who've lost a child know that prayer and know the devastation of watching nothing change.

Psalm 77 opens with someone crying out to God with everything in them—begging him to hear. This isn't a quiet, peaceful prayer; it's a cry from a breaking heart. The psalmist goes on to say things like, "Has God forgotten to be kind?" and "Have his promises permanently failed?" He's wrestling with the same questions many grieving mothers face after unanswered prayers.

I begged God to save Gracie. I prayed for healing with everything I had. And when she died, it felt like every prayer I prayed had fallen flat. For a long time, I avoided talking to God because I didn't know how to face the disappointment. Maybe you carry that same question: *If God could have changed this, why didn't he?*

Psalm 77 gives us permission to name that pain without shame. It shows us that wrestling with unanswered prayer doesn't make you faithless, it makes you human. God doesn't rebuke the psalmist for these questions. He meets him in them.

We may not understand why God didn't give us the miracle we begged for. But Scripture tells us this: Unanswered prayer is not evidence of abandonment. God didn't ignore you; he stayed with you in your breaking, and he has stayed with you every day since.

DAILY PRAYERS

DAY 1 God, I begged you to save my child, and it breaks me that nothing changed. I don't know what to do with this pain. Will you sit with me in this place where disappointment and love collide? Hold me through the questions I can't untangle. Amen.

DAY 2 Lord, it hurts to remember how hard I prayed. I truly believed you would step in. Now I'm left with confusion and disappointment I don't know what to do with. Will you meet me gently today and remind me that you haven't walked away from me or my pain? Amen.

DAY 3 Father, I want to believe that prayer can still bring comfort, even after everything that's happened. Will you give me a moment of peace today; something that helps me feel safe turning toward you again? Show me that you're still a place where my heart can rest. Amen.

DAY 4 God, I don't understand why my child wasn't healed. I asked you for a miracle, and I meant every word. Help me sort through the fear that rises when I think about it. Calm the places that tell me you didn't love us. Speak truth into that ache. Amen.

DAY 5 Lord, when the enemy whispers that my prayers were useless, remind me that you heard every single one. Help me fight the lie that you ignored me. Give me strength to trust that you were holding my child even when my miracle didn't come. Stay close while I wrestle with this. Amen.

DAY 6 Father, I miss my child so much, it's hard to breathe. Sometimes the grief makes me wonder if praying was a waste of time. Will you show me even a small sign of your love today; something that reminds me you're still walking with me through the wreckage? Amen.

DAY 7 God, thank you for being patient with my hurt and my questions. As this week ends, I'm asking you to hold the disappointment that still feels heavy. Teach me how to talk to you again without fear. Help my heart rest in your presence, even without the answers I still long for. Amen.

When Prayer Feels Pointless

When talking to God feels like talking to the air

And though I cry and shout,
he has shut out my prayers.
He has blocked my way with a high stone wall;
he has made my road crooked.

—**Lamentations 3:8–9**

Lamentations was written by Jeremiah, a prophet who watched his entire world fall apart. Jerusalem had been destroyed, families were torn apart, and it looked like God had stepped back and let devastation take over. Jeremiah didn't write this after the worst was over. He wrote it while he was still standing *in* the ruin.

That's why these words hit so hard: "And though I cry and shout, he has shut out my prayers."

Jeremiah wasn't being dramatic; he was being honest. He felt like God wasn't listening. He prayed and nothing changed. He reached out and felt nothing back. If prayer feels pointless to you right now, you are standing exactly where one of Scripture's most faithful men once stood.

I've been there, too. For a long time after Gracie died, I stopped talking to God because it felt useless. I wasn't listening for him, I wasn't talking to him, and honestly, I didn't want to. That silence between us made God feel even farther away. But when I slowly found my way back to prayer, the anger in me started to soften. And little by little, I started to notice him again in tiny, ordinary moments that brought me the smallest pieces of joy.

Jeremiah eventually remembers something true in the middle of his despair: God had not abandoned him. The silence wasn't punishment—it was part of living in a broken, loud world where God sometimes feels quiet.

If prayer feels pointless, you're not broken—you're grieving. And God is still near, even when you can't feel him.

DAILY PRAYERS

DAY 1 God, I don't even know what to say to you right now. Prayer feels empty and I feel unheard. Please meet me in this place where everything feels pointless. I'm tired and hurting, but I'm still reaching for you in the only way I know how today. Amen.

DAY 2 Lord, I feel like my prayers don't make a difference. Nothing changes, and it makes me wonder if you're listening. Will you remind me that my words matter to you? Even the quiet ones? Help me trust that you hear me, even when nothing feels different. Amen.

DAY 3 Father, I've pulled away from you because talking to you feels too heavy. Will you help me find my way back without shame? Show me how to take one small step toward you today and give me a reminder that you're still close. Amen.

DAY 4 God, when I come to you in the ache of missing my child, it feels like I'm talking to the air. Will you show me you're still here? Help me believe that you're present even when you're quiet. I need strength just to keep trying, even when my faith feels thin. Amen.

DAY 5 Lord, the silence makes me doubt myself. Am I praying wrong? Am I doing something wrong? I don't know what else to do. Will you calm that fear? Remind me that silence doesn't mean you're gone. Help me keep reaching for you even when I feel nothing back. Amen.

DAY 6 God, I want to feel you again. Even something small—a moment of peace, a memory of them that doesn't crush me, a breath that comes easier. Will you help me recognize your nearness when it comes? I'm looking; please don't let me miss you. Amen.

DAY 7 Father, thank you for staying close even when I stopped talking. As I go into a new week, help me pray honestly without pressure or guilt. Let prayer feel like connection again, not a chore or a test. And when joy comes in small ways, help me see it as your kindness. Amen.

WEEK 20

God Gave Others What He Didn't Give Me

When other people's blessings make my grief feel sharper

But as for me, I almost lost my footing.
My feet were slipping, and I was almost gone.
For I envied the proud
when I saw them prosper despite their wickedness.

—PSALM 73:2–3

There's a certain kind of pain that rises when you see others receiving what you begged God for. A healthy pregnancy. A baby who comes home. A child who grows up. Even a stroller in a store aisle can make your chest tighten.

You're not angry at them, you're grieving for you. The writer in Psalm 73 admits he "almost lost his footing" because seeing others thrive while he suffered almost destroyed his faith. He wasn't jealous in a petty way—he was grieving what he longed for, what he prayed for, what he didn't get to keep. Loss changes you like that. It sharpens the ache, especially when other people's joy mirrors what you're missing.

After Gracie died, I avoided baby showers, newborn photos, even simple conversations with other moms. Not because I wished anything bad for them but because my heart was raw and everything reminded me of what I lost. You probably carry that same tension—wanting to be glad for others while feeling gutted inside.

Psalm 73 doesn't shame those feelings. It names them honestly. It shows us that God isn't offended when comparison hurts or when someone else's blessing brings your grief to the surface. He sees the weight of what you carry and the unfairness of it all.

If you feel like God gave others what he didn't give you, it doesn't make you ungrateful or bitter. It makes you a mother whose heart still remembers what it held. And God meets you there, steadying you when the ache feels too sharp to name.

DAILY PRAYERS

DAY 1 God, it hurts to watch others receive what I begged you for. I don't want to resent anyone, I'm just sad and tired. Will you sit with me in this ache? Help me bring these feelings to you without shame, and steady me when comparison makes my heart stumble. Amen.

DAY 2 Lord, when I see families smiling or children running, it reminds me of what I'm missing. Will you help me breathe through the ache instead of drowning in it? I don't want to harden my heart, but it hurts so much. Meet me in this tension and hold me close. Amen.

DAY 3 Father, I don't want to feel jealous. I want to celebrate others, but some days it pulls at the deepest part of my grief. Will you take my honesty and bring comfort into it? Show me that you're patient with these feelings and you understand why they rise. Amen.

DAY 4 God, sometimes I wonder why their story looks different from mine. Why their child lived and mine didn't. I know these questions are heavy, but they're real. Please hold my heart as I wrestle. Remind me that you see the full weight of my loss and you haven't forgotten me. Amen.

DAY 5 Lord, protect my heart from bitterness. The enemy would love for this comparison to pull me away from you. Will you help me fight back? Give me strength to release what isn't mine to carry and to feel your nearness in the places where I hurt the most. Amen.

DAY 6 Father, when I feel left out or overlooked, remind me that you haven't kept your love from me. Help me see even a small sign of your kindness today; something that whispers you still care about my hurting heart and will meet me in this longing. Amen.

DAY 7 God, as this week ends, I'm asking for gentleness with myself. Help me hold space for my grief without guilt. When other people's joy feels painful, remind me that you understand. Keep steadying my steps as I learn to live with this ache and still turn toward you. Amen.

When I'm Tired of Being Strong

When I'm exhausted from holding it all together

We were crushed and overwhelmed beyond our ability to endure, and we thought we would never live through it.

—2 Corinthians 1:8

After Gracie died, people told me all the time, "Becky, you're so strong." They meant it kindly, but every time I heard it, something inside me sank. I didn't feel strong. I felt broken. And honestly? What choice did I have besides getting up every day and trying to function? That wasn't strength—it was survival.

As grieving moms, we hear this constantly: "You're strong. You're resilient. You're handling this so well."

But people don't see what it costs us. They don't feel how your chest tightens the moment you step into a room. They don't understand how your body feels heavy from holding in tears. They don't see how pretending to be okay drains you physically in ways you never imagined. This exhaustion doesn't mean you're failing; it means you've been carrying more than anyone realizes.

When Paul writes in 2 Corinthians 1:8 that he was "crushed and overwhelmed beyond his ability to endure," it gives us permission to say those words, too. Even Paul reached the end of what he could carry alone. God never expected you to be the strong one every day.

Maybe what hurts most is wishing someone would look past your brave face and see the tired mom underneath. Maybe you just need permission to be honest. To say, "I'm not strong today," without feeling like you're disappointing anyone.

Here's the truth you're allowed to hold: You don't owe the world strength, you don't have to perform, and you're allowed to be exactly how you are.

God isn't asking you to push through; he simply wants to carry you when you're too exhausted to stand.

DAILY PRAYERS

DAY 1 God, I'm tired of being told I'm strong. I don't feel strong at all—I feel worn down and stretched thin. Will you hold me when I can't keep pushing? Remind me that I don't have to pretend with you. Meet me in this exhaustion and steady my heart. Amen.

DAY 2 Lord, getting through each day feels like climbing a mountain I never trained for. Will you give me the strength I actually need, not the strength people assume I have? Help me take the next small step without feeling like I have to hold everything together alone. Amen.

DAY 3 God, I'm tired of pretending I'm strong. I wish people could see how much this hurts. Will you give me the courage to be honest about where I'm really at? Help me release the pressure to look okay and instead let others in. Remind me that you aren't asking for strength, just truth. Amen.

DAY 4 God, I miss my child so much it hurts to breathe. Some days I collapse under the weight of it. Will you meet me in that collapse instead of expecting me to rise? Let me feel your comfort in the middle of this weakness. Amen.

DAY 5 Lord, I don't want to pretend to be strong anymore. Will you help me be honest with myself and with you? When I feel like I'm falling apart, remind me that you've never asked me to hold myself together. Stay close to me in this tiredness. Amen.

DAY 6 Father, everyone sees the outside version of me—the one who shows up and keeps moving. But you see the inside: the grief, the weariness, the weight. Will you bring the "inside me" moments of rest today? Even small ones. Help me breathe a little easier. Amen.

DAY 7 God, thank you for not expecting strength from me that I don't have. As I enter a new week, help me release the pressure to "bounce back." Teach me to lean on you in real ways, not forced ones. Hold me gently and keep reminding me that weakness isn't failure. Amen.

WEEK 22

Living in a World That No Longer Feels Safe

Living in fear of more loss

The LORD keeps you from all harm
and watches over your life.
The LORD keeps watch over you as you come and go,
both now and forever.

—PSALM 121:7–8

Fear after losing a child doesn't stay small. It follows you everywhere. It shows up when someone doesn't answer their phone, when you hear a siren, when your mind jumps straight to disaster without your permission. Some nights it even follows you into your dreams. After Gracie died, I had dreams of my family members drowning or being hit by a truck, and they were so vivid that I'd wake up shaking. And the fear didn't disappear in the morning; it stayed with me, making the world feel unsafe.

Child loss shatters the belief that life will turn out a certain way. Your brain tries to protect you by imagining everything that could go wrong. It's exhausting, and it makes you feel like danger is everywhere.

Psalm 121 doesn't promise that nothing painful will ever happen; it promises that God watches over your life, that you are never left to walk this unpredictable world alone. For you, that promise might feel complicated because if God watches over your life, why didn't he stop what happened to your child? That question is real, and it deserves honesty. We live in a broken world where tragedy still touches what is precious, and on this side of heaven we will not get all the answers. That's a hard truth to carry.

But this is also true: God didn't abandon your child and he hasn't abandoned you. You might still feel scared, but it doesn't mean you're unguarded. God watches over your life with a care that's deeper than fear, and he walks with you through every uncertain step.

DAILY PRAYERS

DAY 1 God, I wake up most days already bracing for something bad to happen. Losing my child made everything feel uncertain. Will you steady my heart today? Remind me that you see me and that you watch over my life even when fear tries to convince me otherwise. Amen.

DAY 2 Lord, sometimes I'm terrified that more loss is coming. My mind goes straight to the worst that can happen. Is this normal, God? Will you calm the trauma that keeps stirring up in me? Help me remember that you're present and that fear doesn't have the final word over my days. Amen.

DAY 3 Father, the anxiety hits without warning, and my mind spirals before I can stop it. Will you take some of this worry from me? Remind me that I don't have to fear tomorrow. Help me breathe, stay present, and trust that you'll walk with me into whatever comes. Amen.

DAY 4 God, sometimes the nightmares feel too real. I wake up imagining I've lost more people in my life, and it follows me through the day. Will you break the grip that fear has on my mind? Will you give me moments of peace that remind me you're still watching over the people I love? Amen.

DAY 5 Lord, I know the enemy loves to use fear to keep me anxious and distracted. Will you help me fight back? Will you remind me that you haven't abandoned me? Give me the strength to choose truth over fear and courage over the lies that try to control my heart. Amen.

DAY 6 Father, I'm afraid of losing more than I already have. Sometimes I even worry something will happen to me, and it leaves me feeling exposed. Will you protect my life, God? Help me trust that you're near and paying attention, even when I can't feel safe on my own. Amen.

DAY 7 God, I want to live without constantly scanning for danger. I want to remember my child without fear swallowing me whole. Will you help me move through the world with a little more ease? Show me signs of your care today. Teach my heart that I am not walking this alone. Amen.

When I Need a Sign

When I hope God will show up in a small way

"Ask the Lord your God for a sign of confirmation, Ahaz. Make it as difficult as you want—as high as heaven or as deep as the place of the dead."

—Isaiah 7:11

Some days, grief makes you whisper, "God, I need to know you're here—please show me." Nothing dramatic; just a reminder, enough to steady you for another day.

In Isaiah 7, King Ahaz felt overwhelmed by what he was facing: two nations threatening his people. Instead of shaming him, God did something unexpected: He invited Ahaz to ask for a sign. "Make it as difficult as you want," God told him, knowing how deeply Ahaz needed reassurance. Ahaz refused to ask, but God sent a sign anyway. The promise of a child who would be called *Immanuel*, meaning "God is with us." It was God's way of saying, "You are not alone, even now."

After Gracie passed, I found myself asking for signs all the time. Not big ones; just something small to remind me heaven is close. And God met me in ways I didn't expect, like a stranger saying her name, a butterfly or a pink sunset on a hard day, a verse that felt written for me in the exact right moment.

People call them "God winks," but for a grieving parent, they're more like lifelines. Asking for reassurance doesn't mean your faith is weak. It means your heart is hurting, and the same God who offered Ahaz a sign still offers gentle mercy when you need it most.

DAILY PRAYERS

DAY 1 God, I'm tired, and I miss my child so deeply it hurts to breathe. Will you show me something today that helps me feel your nearness? Even something small? Remind me that I'm not forgotten and that you still see me and the ache I carry. Amen.

DAY 2 Lord, sometimes I feel silly for needing a sign. But you know how fragile my heart feels without my child here. Will you meet me anyway? I'm paying attention, God. Please make your presence clear to me. Amen.

DAY 3 Father, I'm not looking for proof, just comfort. Some days I wonder if you're still close or if my grief has pushed you away. Will you remind me you're here? Let something reach my heart today that feels personal and unmistakably from you. Amen.

DAY 4 God, I miss my child so much. Will you speak to me through something familiar—a color, a moment, a memory—anything that reminds me I'm not walking this grief alone? Help me recognize the ways you're still moving in my life. Amen.

DAY 5 Lord, on days when I feel overlooked, will you remind me that you haven't turned your face from me? I long for a sign that you still notice my tears and the space my child once filled. Calm my doubts and steady my heart as only you can do. Amen.

DAY 6 Father, I'm watching and listening for you. I want you to meet me in this place. Will you help my heart stay open? Will you send me comfort, no matter how small, and help me recognize it and receive it without questioning whether I'm worthy of it? Amen.

DAY 7 God, thank you for understanding why I need reassurance. Will you send a sign today that reminds me my child is safe with you and that I am still held, too? Let your nearness feel real enough to quiet the ache for just a moment. Amen.

WEEK 24

Learning to Trust God Again

How do I trust God after this?

Trust in the LORD with all your heart;
do not depend on your own understanding.
Seek his will in all you do,
and he will show you which path to take.

—**PROVERBS 3:5–6**

Proverbs 3:5–6 is probably a verse you've heard more times than you can count. Maybe it hung on a wall in your home growing up or showed up in cards people sent after your child died, but most of us never think about this verse through the eyes of grief and through a heart that trusted God once and now isn't sure how to do that anymore.

"Trust in the LORD with all your heart; do not depend on your own understanding." Those words hit differently after loss because nothing makes sense anymore. Nothing feels steady, and trusting with "all your heart" feels impossible when your heart is shattered.

This verse isn't asking you to ignore your reality, and it isn't telling you to pretend you're okay. It's actually an invitation to release what is too heavy to carry alone. "Do not depend on your own understanding" becomes less of a command and more of a lifeline. It means: You don't have to figure this out. You're not expected to understand why your child died. God knows you can't make sense of this, and he isn't waiting for you to.

What does trust look like now, though? Maybe it's letting God hold the pieces of your life you don't know how to manage. Maybe it's taking the next breath and asking him to guide your steps because you don't recognize yourself anymore. Maybe it's whispering, "I want to trust you, but I need help."

This verse isn't about perfect trust; it's about letting God lead you when you don't know which way to go.

DAILY PRAYERS

DAY 1 God, trusting you feels different now. Losing my child rewired everything inside me. Will you help me take even one small step toward you today? Show me how to lean on you when nothing makes sense. I don't need certainty, just your steady hand somewhere in this fog. Amen.

DAY 2 Lord, I don't know how to trust when my heart is broken. What does trust even look like now? Will you teach me gently? Remind me I don't have to understand everything to be held by you. Help me believe you won't let go of me even when I'm unsure. Amen.

DAY 3 Father, I miss my child so much that trusting anything feels risky. Will you help me rest in your care even with my fear still present? Hold my heart in the places that doubt the most. Guide my next steps when I can't see the path clearly. Amen.

DAY 4 God, my understanding ends quickly these days. I can't make sense of my child's absence or the life I'm living now. Will you carry what I cannot? Teach me to trust you with the pieces I don't know how to hold. Let your presence steady me through this uncertainty. Amen.

DAY 5 Lord, trusting you used to feel easier. Now I'm trying to rebuild something I never expected to lose. Will you meet me halfway? Show me reminders of your goodness that are small enough for my hurting heart to hold. Help me believe you're guiding me even when I can't feel it. Amen.

DAY 6 Father, some days I'm scared to trust because I don't want to be hurt again. Will you reassure me that trusting you isn't risky? Calm the parts of me that brace for more loss. Teach me to lean on you without fearing what tomorrow might bring. I need your steadfastness. Amen.

DAY 7 God, thank you for staying patient with me as I learn to trust again. I don't have this figured out, but I want to keep trying. Will you walk with me into this new week? Guide each step, quiet my questions, and hold my heart as I follow you one breath at a time. Amen.

WEEK 25

Choosing Surrender Over Control

When control feels like the only safety I have left

Then Jesus said, "Come to me, all of you who are weary and carry heavy burdens, and I will give you rest. Take my yoke upon you. Let me teach you, because I am humble and gentle at heart, and you will find rest for your souls."

—MATTHEW 11:28–29

After your child dies, control becomes a kind of shield. You hold tightly to anything you can predict or manage because you know what it feels like for your whole world to collapse without warning. People may tell you to "trust God," but they don't understand how loss rewires your instincts. Control doesn't come from pride—it comes from trauma.

Jesus's words in Matthew 11 aren't a command to stop trying, they're an invitation to rest. "Come to me, all of you who are weary and carry heavy burdens, and I will give you rest." Surrender isn't about letting go of everything, it's about letting God carry what was never yours to hold.

After Gracie died, I clung to control anywhere I could find it. If something felt even a little unpredictable, I acted fast because losing control terrified me. It reminded me of the day everything fell apart and I couldn't do anything to stop it. So I tried to manage every detail, every possibility, every scenario—not because I wanted control but because I didn't trust myself to survive another disaster.

But Jesus doesn't ask us to surrender from a place of strength; he invites us to surrender from exhaustion. He knows how fear tries to run our lives after loss, and he doesn't shame us for tightening our grip.

Surrender isn't a single moment—it's slowly learning to let God carry the weight you were never meant to hold and releasing one thing at a time. Bring him what feels too heavy.

DAILY PRAYERS

DAY 1 God, I've been gripping everything so tightly because I'm scared of what might happen if I don't. Losing my child taught me how fast life can fall apart. Will you take some of what I'm carrying today? I'm tired, and I need help loosening my grip. Amen.

DAY 2 Lord, surrender feels risky and I don't want to be caught off guard again, but I also don't want to live in fear. Will you show me what it looks like to rest in you? Help me trust you with one small thing today; just one. Amen.

DAY 3 Father, I miss my child so much that the world feels unsafe. When I feel the urge to control every detail, will you calm my heart? Remind me that you are near, that not everything depends on me, and that I can breathe without bracing for disaster. Amen.

DAY 4 God, sometimes I jump into action the second I feel things slipping. It feels automatic now. Will you meet me in that panic? Help me pause long enough to remember I don't have to hold everything together. Teach me how to let you carry what I can't. Amen.

DAY 5 Lord, you see the fear underneath my need for control. Will you speak into that fear today? Help me lay down at least one worry, one burden, one expectation. Show me that surrender isn't losing—it's letting you help me when my own strength runs out. Amen.

DAY 6 Father, I don't always trust myself to handle another heartbreak. When I'm bracing for something bad to happen, will you steady me? Remind me that surrender doesn't mean pretending—it means letting you meet me right where I'm scared. Hold my heart in the places that feel fragile. Amen.

DAY 7 God, thank you for being patient with me while I learn how to release what overwhelms me. I want to lean on you more than my own fear. Will you walk with me into this new week and help me choose rest over control, even if it's one moment at a time? Amen.

Learning to Live in God's Ongoing Healing

Letting go of the pressure to be "healed"

And I am certain that God, who began the good work within you, will continue his work until it is finally finished on the day when Christ Jesus returns.

—PHILIPPIANS 1:6

If you're anything like me, you've probably had people tell you, "You'll heal with time," as if there's some finish line you're supposed to cross. But when you've lost a child, "healed" can feel like a dismissive word. It can sound like an expectation to be over something you'll carry forever.

Philippians 1:6 paints a different picture. It says God began a good work in you and he will continue that work until the day you are with Jesus. That means you are not a project he expects to finish quickly—you are someone he is gently and patiently tending.

There's a difference between healed and healing. Healed sounds final—like your grieving should be done by now. Healing is actually ongoing. It makes room for tears years later, for setbacks after stretches of calm, for moments that still knock the wind out of you. It honors that your love for your child hasn't ended, so of course, the ache hasn't, either.

After Gracie died, I wondered what was wrong with me because I wasn't "getting better." I can see now that God was and is still working in me quietly and constantly in ways I didn't recognize at the time.

You are not failing because you are still hurting. You are living in the middle of a work God hasn't finished yet, and he promises he will not stop until the day he makes you whole in his presence, with your child *again*.

DAILY PRAYERS

DAY 1 God, I feel pressure to be "better," but I'm nowhere near that. Will you remind me that healing isn't a race? Help me breathe without feeling like I'm failing. Hold the parts of me that still ache for my child, and walk with me in the slow work you're doing. Amen.

DAY 2 Lord, some days it feels like I'm moving backward instead of forward. Will you stay with me in the places that still hurt? Help me release the idea that I should be further along. Teach me to trust that you're working in me even when I can't see any change. Amen.

DAY 3 Father, I miss my child so much. Some moments still drop me to my knees. Please remind me that this ache doesn't mean I'm broken beyond repair. Show me how to live in the "still healing" place without shame. Meet me with gentleness when my heart feels thin. Amen.

DAY 4 Lord, when people say things that make it seem like my grief should be over, help me not to crumble under their words. Give me strength to protect my heart and wisdom to know what to let in. Teach me how to live without needing anyone else's timeline for my healing. Amen.

DAY 5 Lord, when I start comparing my healing to someone else's, will you pull me back? My story is different because my child is different. Help me trust that you know what my heart needs. Give me courage to move at the pace that honors my grief, not others' expectations. Amen.

DAY 6 God, some days healing feels impossible. I still have moments where missing my child knocks the breath out of me. Will you steady me when those waves come? Teach me that healing doesn't mean forgetting and help me feel your presence in the middle of what still feels unfinished. Amen.

DAY 7 Father, thank you for the small ways you've carried me this week. I know I'm still healing and may always be but I'm grateful you're in every step. Will you keep shaping me and helping me live this life without my child while I hold their memory close? Amen.

PART 3

Who Am I Now? Motherhood in the Shadow of Loss

WEEK 27

Still a Mother

Do I still count as a mom?

"Never! Can a mother forget her nursing child?
Can she feel no love for the child she has borne?
But even if that were possible,
I would not forget you!"

—**Isaiah 49:15**

One of the deepest wounds after losing a child is the quiet question you rarely say out loud: *Am I still a mother?*

People stop saying your child's name. Forms ask for the number of children you have. Strangers make comments that leave you frozen between honesty and the fear of making someone uncomfortable. And inside, you feel the ache of a role that didn't end, even though others act like it did.

Isaiah 49:15 shows us how God sees motherhood: as something so fierce and unbreakable that he uses it to explain his own love. "Can a mother forget her child?" he asks. The assumed answer is no—because a mother's love isn't erased by death, distance, or time. Even if the world forgets, he says, *I won't.*

You are still a mother because your love didn't end. Your child's life didn't evaporate when their heartbeat stopped. They existed, they mattered, and they are known by God. The bond you formed didn't unravel; it changed form, but it didn't disappear.

When Gracie died, I struggled with this, too. People stopped mentioning her, and I wondered if my identity as her mom would slowly fade away. But God reminded me: Motherhood isn't measured by who can see it. It's written in love, memory, and scar tissue. It's part of who you are. And it is honored by him.

God still calls you "mother"—not past tense, not former, but *beloved mother of the child he has not forgotten.*

DAILY PRAYERS

DAY 1 God, some days I wonder if I'm allowed to call myself a mother when my child isn't here. Will you remind me that love is what makes me a mom, not the length of their life? Hold my heart when the world forgets the title you still give me. Amen.

DAY 2 Lord, when people look at me and don't see a mother, it hurts in ways I can't explain. Will you help me hold on to the truth that you see the love I carry every day? Show me that motherhood doesn't disappear just because others can't see it. Amen.

DAY 3 Father, I miss my child so deeply that it feels like a part of me is missing, too. Remind me that my bond with them didn't end; it just changed. When doubts creep in, whisper to my heart that I am still theirs and they are still mine. Amen.

DAY 4 God, it's hard when people stop saying my child's name. It makes me feel like my role as a mother is fading. Will you bring people into my life who aren't afraid to acknowledge my child? And when no one else does, help me feel your assurance that I'm still their mom today and always. Amen.

DAY 5 Lord, some days I feel invisible, like my motherhood lives only inside me. Will you give me courage to honor my child in small ways, even when others don't understand? Keep reminding me that this role you gave me is real, enduring, and held safely in your hands. Amen.

DAY 6 Father, the silence around my child's life can make me question everything. Will you steady my heart? Restore the part of me that feels forgotten. Show me in gentle, unmistakable ways that you remember my child, and you remember me as their mother. That truth matters more than anything. Amen.

DAY 7 God, thank you that my motherhood isn't defined by what I can hold, but by who I love. Thank you for seeing every tear, every memory, every ache that proves I am still a mom. As I enter a new week, help me walk in that truth with tenderness and strength. Amen.

Answering "Do You Have Kids?"

Navigating the pain and pressure inside the question "Do you have kids?"

"I don't have a husband," the woman replied. Jesus said, "You're right! You don't have a husband—for you have had five husbands, and you aren't even married to the man you're living with now. You certainly spoke the truth!"

—John 4:17–18

This might seem like a strange verse for a devotional written to bereaved mothers, but stay with me—because what happens in this moment between Jesus and the Samaritan woman mirrors the emotional tightrope you walk every time someone asks, "Do you have kids?"

It seems like such an innocent question. But for a grieving mother, it carries pain, pressure, guilt, and an immediate inner scramble: *Do I protect my heart or do I tell the truth and risk breaking open in front of someone who may not understand?*

In John 4, Jesus asks the woman a deeply personal question. She gives the safest version of the truth: "I don't have a husband." It's not the whole story—it's the part she can manage. And instead of correcting her or demanding more, Jesus responds with compassion. He already knows her full truth. He sees her history, her heartbreak, and the weight behind her answer.

That's the comfort here: God knows the whole truth about you, too. When someone asks if you have kids, he sees the child you're thinking of. He sees the hesitation, the ache, the love you carry. He sees the guilt you feel no matter how you answer.

You don't betray your child by protecting your heart. You don't owe the world your deepest wound. Whether you say "yes," "no," or something in between, God holds the fuller story with tenderness.

And nothing—not your answer, not someone's reaction—can change the truth: *You are still their mother.*

DAILY PRAYERS

DAY 1 God, you know how much this question takes out of me. Every time someone asks, I feel the ache all over again. Will you give me wisdom in the moment? Help me answer in the way my heart can handle, without guilt, and remind me that you see the child I'm thinking of. Amen.

DAY 2 Lord, when I choose the safer answer, I walk away feeling like I failed my child. Will you lift that guilt from me? You know the truth I carry. Teach me that protecting my heart doesn't discredit my motherhood. Please help me feel your compassion instead of shame. Amen.

DAY 3 Father, some days I want to tell the full story and other days I can barely breathe when the question comes. Will you guide my words? Help me recognize when honesty is healing and when silence is necessary. Hold my heart either way and remind me that you never forget my child. Amen.

DAY 4 God, it hurts when people don't understand why this question is so painful. Will you surround me with people who speak gently, who ask thoughtfully, who hold space for my motherhood? And when that doesn't happen, steady me with the truth that you see the love behind my hesitation. Amen.

DAY 5 Lord, the world doesn't see my motherhood, but you do. You see the love I carry, the memories, the longing that never goes away. When I feel invisible, will you remind me that I am known by you? Help me rest in the identity you've given me as my child's mother. Amen.

DAY 6 Father, sometimes I wish I didn't have to think so hard about a question that should be simple. Will you ease the pressure I put on myself? Help me breathe in those moments and remember that I can answer differently on different days. Give me grace for how it changes from day to day. Amen.

DAY 7 God, thank you for seeing every part of my story—the words I say and the ones I swallow. As another week begins, teach me to carry my motherhood with tenderness, honesty, and strength. Help me trust that no question, moment, or answer can erase my child from your heart or mine. Amen.

WEEK 29

When Grief Gets Compared

Letting God define the weight of my loss, not other people

Jesus replied, "If I want him to remain alive until I return, what is that to you? As for you, follow me."

—JOHN 21:22

Comparison shows up in grief, especially among bereaved mothers. Sometimes it sounds gentle, even well meaning: "Oh, but your loss was so much harder than mine." When I hear that, something in me aches. Not because my pain needs defending but because another mother's pain is quietly minimized. A child lost is a child lost. The circumstances don't change the weight.

When grief is compared, pain starts getting measured instead of honored. Mothers then wonder if their grief is valid, if it's enough, if they're allowed to hurt as deeply as they do. Comparison creates a scale God never designed.

In John 21, Peter has just been restored by Jesus after denying him. Then Peter looks at John and asks, "What about him, Lord?" In other words, how will his story compare to mine? Jesus doesn't explain or justify. He redirects. "What is that to you? As for you, follow me."

We notice how long another mother had with her child, how public her grief is, how people respond to her pain. Sometimes others even do the comparing for us, ranking losses without realizing the harm. Jesus's words cut through that noise. Faithfulness doesn't come from understanding someone else's path, but from staying present in your own.

God does not rank grief. Each child mattered fully. Each loss is heavy in its own way. You don't need comparison to validate your pain. Jesus's invitation is simple and hard: Stay with your story and stay with him.

DAILY PRAYERS

DAY 1 God, when grief starts getting measured, help me step away from the scale. Teach me to honor my child and my loss without defending either. Amen.

DAY 2 Father, sometimes comparison sneaks in before I realize it. I start wondering if I'm allowed to hurt this much. Will you remind me that you see my grief clearly, without ranking or judgment? Help me rest in that truth today. Amen.

DAY 3 God, when others compare losses, I don't always know how to respond. Give me wisdom to disengage without guilt. Help me trust that I don't owe anyone an explanation for my pain. Amen.

DAY 4 Lord, protect my heart when conversations start measuring grief. I don't want my pain or another mother's pain minimized. Help me hold compassion without comparison and remember that every child matters fully to you. Amen.

DAY 5 Father, I notice myself comparing stories, timelines, and circumstances. Please stop me gently when I do. Help me stay rooted in my own story. Amen.

DAY 6 God, when comparison makes me question if my grief is enough, remind me of the truth. My child mattered. My love was real. My loss is heavy. Help me believe that without needing anyone else to agree. Amen.

DAY 7 Lord, let me follow you instead of comparing myself to others. As I move into another week, help me stay present in my own story. Give me the courage to honor my child without measuring my grief against anyone else's. Amen.

WEEK 30

When Motherhood Feels Invisible

Being a mother when the world doesn't see it

Thereafter, Hagar used another name to refer to the LORD, who had spoken to her. She said, "You are the God who sees me." She also said, "Have I truly seen the One who sees me?"

—GENESIS 16:13

Hagar didn't just feel alone; she felt unseen. She had carried a child, endured pain, and then found herself pushed to the margins. In that place, she names God as "the God who sees me." Not the God who fixed everything but the God who noticed.

After your child dies, feeling invisible can feel especially raw. You are still a mother, but the world doesn't always treat you like one. You aren't invited to the mom group. You don't get asked about your children the same way. Conversations change or stop altogether. And sometimes the hardest part isn't knowing God sees you; it's wanting other people to see you, too.

That longing is not wrong.

Wanting your motherhood to be acknowledged doesn't mean you're seeking attention. It means you want your child to be real in the world, not only in your heart.

Genesis 16:13 doesn't shame Hagar for naming her pain. And God doesn't shame you for wanting to be recognized, either. He sees the disappointment of being left out. He sees the sting of invisibility. He sees you wondering where you fit now.

You may not always know what to do with that ache. Sometimes it helps to choose people who can sit with your story instead of avoiding it. And sometimes the most honest prayer is simply *I want to be seen. I want my child to be remembered.*

Even when the world doesn't see your motherhood, it still exists. It still matters. And it is fully known by God.

DAILY PRAYERS

DAY 1 God, some days it hurts to feel invisible in a role that defines my whole heart. I am still a mother, even when no one acknowledges it. Please remind me today that my love didn't disappear with my child. You see it. You see me. Amen.

DAY 2 Father, I ache for my motherhood to be acknowledged, even when others don't know how to see it. Loving my child shaped my life and that still matters. When this longing rises, what do you want me to do with it? Help me bring it to you honestly. Amen.

DAY 3 God, I want my motherhood to be visible, not hidden or tiptoed around. When my child goes unmentioned and I feel erased, please notice me there. Give me courage to exist honestly, even when others don't know how to respond. Remind me that my story still deserves space. Amen.

DAY 4 Lord, sometimes I feel left out of spaces I once belonged in. I wonder where I fit now. Please meet me in that uncertainty and remind me that my place as a mother is not erased by loss. Help me feel like I belong again. Amen.

DAY 5 God, would you send me someone who sees me as a mother? Someone who doesn't look away. Someone who lets my child be real in conversation. I'm tired of carrying this alone. Please bring connection that feels safe and kind. Amen.

DAY 6 Father, when I want acknowledgment but feel ashamed for wanting it, remind me that this desire comes from love. Help me stop minimizing my pain. Teach me that longing to be seen is not weakness—it is grief asking to be held. Amen.

DAY 7 God, thank you for seeing what others miss. As I move through this week, help me rest in the truth that my motherhood still matters. Hold both my love and my loneliness with care. Stay close when the world forgets. Amen.

Carrying My Child's Legacy

Understanding how your child's life still speaks

It was by faith that Abel brought a more acceptable offering to God than Cain did. . . . Although Abel is long dead, he still speaks to us by his example of faith.

—Hebrews 11:4

Abel's life was short—painfully short. Scripture doesn't tell us much about him, only that he brought God an offering with a sincere heart. His parents lived through the nightmare no parent imagines: burying their child.

And yet Hebrews says something astonishing: "Abel still speaks." His life still speaks because God preserved his story, showing the worth he places on a life the world might overlook or forget.

That truth has always moved me, because it echoes what so many grieving mothers wonder: My child was here . . . but will anyone remember? Will their life matter beyond the short time I had them?

After Gracie died, carrying her legacy became the one thing I could still do. I started Cakes From Grace for cardiac kids like her, and now I honor her through the books I write. But please hear this gently: Your child's legacy does not depend on a nonprofit or a platform.

Your child's legacy lives in you. In how their existence reshaped you. In the tenderness that deepened your heart. In the strength you never wanted but now carry. In the ache that shows how fiercely they were loved. In the way you see the world differently because they were here.

Legacy isn't measured by years lived or milestones reached. Legacy is measured by love—and love always leaves a mark.

Just like Abel, your child's life still speaks. Not necessarily through accomplishments but through the God who remembers them, the love that formed you, and the story he continues to honor, even now.

DAILY PRAYERS

DAY 1 God, some days I wonder how to honor my child without feeling crushed by the weight of missing them. Will you show me what it looks like to carry their memory gently? Help me see the small ways their life is still shaping mine, even when no one else notices. Amen.

DAY 2 Lord, I feel the pressure to make my child's life "mean something," and it exhausts me. Please free me from expectations that aren't from you. Teach me that legacy isn't performance—it's love. Help me trust that the way I carry them in my heart is already enough. Amen.

DAY 3 Father, when I worry their life will be forgotten, remind me that you never forget. Their story is safe with you. Take away the fear that I'm the only one who remembers. Let me find comfort in knowing their life mattered to you long before it mattered to anyone else. Amen.

DAY 4 God, thank you for walking with me as I carry my child's story. Will you keep teaching me how to do this with honesty and grace? Help me remember that their impact isn't measured by what I create, but by the love that lives in me because of them. Amen.

DAY 5 Lord, thank you for the parts of me that changed because my child existed. Will you help me see those changes as gifts instead of wounds? Show me how their life continues to grow something good in me, even in places still tender. Help me trust that transformation. Amen.

DAY 6 Father, on days when I wonder if I'm honoring my child "the right way," remind me there isn't one right way. Help me release comparison. Guide me toward whatever reflects love, not pressure. Lead me gently as I learn what carrying their legacy looks like today. Amen.

DAY 7 God, as another week ends, I thank you for the ways my child's life still shapes mine. When I doubt their impact, remind me that you don't forget what I treasure. Help me walk forward carrying their legacy with hope, gentleness, and truth. Let their love continue to change me. Amen.

WEEK 32

Mothering from Heaven's Side

How do I still mother my child when they're in heaven?

But we are citizens of heaven, where the Lord Jesus Christ lives. And we are eagerly waiting for him to return as our Savior.

—PHILIPPIANS 3:20

When your child is in heaven, the word *mother* can suddenly feel confusing. You still feel like their mom—fully, fiercely—but the ways you were supposed to care for them were taken from you. The routines, the purpose, the everyday ways you planned to show up . . . they vanished. Now you're left asking a question no mother imagines: *How do I mother a child I can't hold anymore?*

Philippians 3:20 gives us an anchor: "We are citizens of heaven, where the Lord Jesus Christ lives." Your child has not gone into nothingness. They are home. They belong to the same Savior who holds you together here. Heaven isn't far away—it's the place your child is fully alive, fully safe, fully known.

So what does mothering look like now? It's remembering them without apologizing. It's saying their name. It's celebrating their birthday. It's keeping something close that reminds you of them. It's living differently because their life changed yours.

After Gracie died, I longed for people to ask about her—even strangers. I wanted any excuse to say her name. For years, I searched for a way to invite those conversations. Eventually, I tattooed her name on my forearm, "Gracia" (which is her given name). People ask about it all the time. And I get to tell them it's my daughter's name. She lived. She mattered. She still does.

You don't have to get a tattoo. Your child's legacy is carried in you. Mothering didn't end—it changed. You are still their mom, and every way you remember and love them is seen by heaven and held by God.

DAILY PRAYERS

DAY 1 God, it's hard to know what it means to be a mother now. My arms feel empty, but my heart is still full of them. Will you show me how to love them from here? Teach me that my motherhood didn't end; it just changed. Help me feel connected to them today. Amen.

DAY 2 Lord, sometimes I feel lost without the tasks and routines that were supposed to come with mothering my child. What do I do with this love now? Please guide me toward small, gentle ways to honor my child. Help me see that remembering them is an act of mothering. Amen.

DAY 3 Father, I miss saying my child's name out loud. It aches in me. Will you provide moments where I can speak about them without fear? Give me courage to share who they are to me and remind me that talking about them keeps their love close. Amen.

DAY 4 God, sometimes I feel weird for needing something tangible to hold, to wear, to see. But these small things make me feel like their mom again. Will you bless the ways I keep them close? Let each one remind me that my connection to them is real and not broken. Amen.

DAY 5 Lord, I often wonder if my child knows how much I still love them. Will you carry that love to them in ways I can't? Take away the fear that I'm failing them from here. Show me that our love is still held between us—unchanged by distance, unchanged by death. Amen.

DAY 6 God, the world sees motherhood as something physical—diapers, lunches, milestones. But my motherhood lives in memories, longing, love, and the ache of missing them. Please remind me that you see the mother I am, even when others don't. Amen.

DAY 7 Father, as I face another week without my child, help me feel the ways I am still connected to them. Teach me to notice the gentle reminders you place in my path. Let every memory, every tear, every whisper of their name feel like a part of how I mother them now. Amen.

When My Family Feels Incomplete

Living with what's missing

Yet I am confident I will see the LORD's goodness
while I am here in the land of the living.
Wait patiently for the LORD.
Be brave and courageous.
Yes, wait patiently for the LORD.

—PSALM 27:13–14

After loss, your family doesn't just change—it feels unfinished. There is a space that will never be filled the way you imagined. It shows up in photos, at holidays, in conversations, and in the life you thought you were building. Even if others still see "a family," you feel the missing piece every day.

Psalm 27:13–14 says something bold in the middle of that ache: "I will see the Lord's goodness while I am here in the land of the living." Not only in heaven. Not only someday. *Here.*

But then David says, "Wait patiently." He is not waiting for the missing piece to return. He is not waiting for the ache to disappear. He is waiting for God's goodness to meet him inside a life that no longer looks the way he planned.

That goodness may not look like restoration. It may look like peace. Peace that lets you sit at the table without collapsing. Peace that lets you hold joy and sorrow in the same breath. Peace that doesn't fix the emptiness but makes it survivable.

When your family feels incomplete, you are not waiting for your story to rewind itself. You are waiting for God to teach you how to live faithfully with what it looks like now.

Peace often comes quietly—through repetition, honesty, and permission to grieve without fixing what was broken.

And that quiet steadiness—that ability to keep going—may be the goodness you begin to see here, in the land of the living.

DAILY PRAYERS

DAY 1 God, my family looks different now, and I feel what's missing every day. Some days I barely recognize this life. Meet me here. Remind me that you are present in this version of my story, not just the one I hoped for. Stay close inside the ache. Amen.

DAY 2 Lord, this loss has changed the shape of my family, and I don't always know how to hold that. Teach me how to live inside what feels unfinished without rushing to fix it. Help me give myself permission to grieve what was and what might have been. Amen.

DAY 3 Father, some days the future feels heavy and unclear. I don't know what my family will look like from here. Will you steady me in the waiting? Help me trust you with what I cannot see yet and give me peace for today, not answers for tomorrow. Amen.

DAY 4 God, I feel the weight of what's missing in quiet moments and loud ones. Please help me carry this without letting it crush me. Show me how to honor my child and my family's story while still finding ways to breathe and live again. Amen.

DAY 5 Lord, I'm learning that waiting itself can hurt. Waiting for clarity, for peace, for my fear to ease. Will you sit with me and my family in this in-between place? Help me believe that you are working even when nothing seems to be changing. Amen.

DAY 6 Father, I don't want to compare my family to what others have or to what I once imagined. Free me from that pressure. Teach me how to live gently inside my reality and remind me that my family's story still matters, even with its gaps and grief. Amen.

DAY 7 God, as another week begins, I bring you my family just as it is—incomplete, tender, and loved. Help me trust you in the waiting. Will you hold for me what feels fragile? Stay close as we learn how to live this life we didn't choose, one day at a time. Amen.

WEEK 34

Finding Purpose Again

Living when the life I prepared for is gone

"For I know the plans I have for you," says the LORD. "They are plans for good and not for disaster, to give you a future and a hope. In those days when you pray, I will listen. If you look for me wholeheartedly, you will find me."

—**JEREMIAH 29:11–13**

After your child dies, purpose doesn't just feel unclear—it feels stolen. You were supposed to be caring for them, building a life around their needs, watching them grow. That was your direction, your reason. When they're gone, the question isn't philosophical. It's practical and aching: *What am I supposed to do now?*

Jeremiah's words were written to people living in the aftermath of loss, not the resolution of it. Their homes were gone. Their future plans had collapsed. God didn't give them a clear roadmap or new assignment. He told them to pray, seek him, and trust that he was still working even while nothing made sense. That waiting is brutal.

After Gracie died, I kept searching for purpose like it was something I could finally "get right." I thought I had found it, only to feel God asking me to pivot. A nonprofit. Then pivot again. Write a book. Even now, I know it may change again. That used to frustrate me. I wanted certainty, something solid that wouldn't shift beneath my feet.

Purpose after loss is not a straight line. It's a willingness to keep walking in the direction God seems to be leading, even when it's slow, unclear, and exhausting. You aren't failing when the path changes. You're responding.

If you're tired of trying to figure it all out, God's not disappointed in you. He isn't asking you to have it nailed down. He's asking you to keep showing up, to keep praying, to keep listening, even when the waiting feels endless.

Purpose unfolds over time. Sometimes painfully slowly. And God stays with you through every turn.

DAILY PRAYERS

DAY 1 God, I don't know what I'm supposed to do with my life now. The role I prepared for is gone, and I feel lost without it. Please meet me here. Sit with me in the confusion and remind me that my worth and purpose didn't disappear with my child. Amen.

DAY 2 Lord, the waiting feels endless and exhausting. I keep asking what you want from me, and I hear nothing back. Will you help me stay here without panicking? Teach me how to wait without feeling forgotten. I need you to hold me steady when purpose feels far away. Amen.

DAY 3 Father, I've tried to follow where I thought you were leading, and then everything changed again. I'm tired of pivoting. I'm tired of starting over. Please remind me that changing direction doesn't mean I failed. Help me trust that you are still guiding me, even now. Amen.

DAY 4 God, some days I'm afraid I'll never feel useful again. I miss having something clear to wake up for. Please show me that my life still matters, even in this in-between space. Help me believe that waiting does not mean I am wasting my life. Amen.

DAY 5 Lord, I want certainty, but you keep asking me to trust you instead. Why is this so hard? Why can't I just know what comes next? Give me courage to keep walking without having all the answers. Stay close when the lack of clarity makes me want to give up. Amen.

DAY 6 Father, I feel pressure to have everything figured out, as if I should already know who I am becoming and what will bring joy again. Please take that pressure off me. Help me move at your pace, not anyone else's. Be gentle with my questions and my slow becoming. Amen.

DAY 7 God, as I begin another week, I don't have clarity, but I'm still here. I'm still listening. I'm still willing. Please keep guiding me one step at a time. Help me trust that purpose can unfold slowly, and that you are walking with me through every uncertain turn. Amen.

Letting Go of the Old Me

When the old me is gone, too

We put away our harps,
hanging them on the branches of poplar trees.
For our captors demanded a song from us.
Our tormentors insisted on a joyful hymn:
"Sing us one of those songs of Jerusalem!"
But how can we sing the songs of the LORD
while in a pagan land?

—**PSALM 137:2–4**

Psalm 137 gives language to a kind of grief that doesn't get talked about enough. The people aren't just mourning what they lost, they're mourning who they were before everything changed. "We put away our harps," they say. Not because they forgot how to play but because they no longer had the capacity for joy. The songs that once fit their lives no longer matched their reality.

After your child dies, this can feel painfully familiar. You're not only grieving them. You're grieving the version of yourself who existed before the loss. The woman who felt lighter. The one who didn't wake up tired. The one who made plans without calculating how much grief she could carry that day. She's gone, too, and that loss matters.

Then the psalm says something even harder: "They demanded a song." The world expects you to cope, to smile, to show strength, to function as if this life still makes sense. People may not mean harm, but the pressure to be resilient is there.

And the response cuts straight to the heart: "How can we sing the songs of the LORD while in a pagan land?" In other words, *I don't know how to live here without my child.*

God does not correct that question. He allows it to be spoken.

If you feel angry that you're still here living a life you didn't choose, you are not alone. Grieving the old you doesn't mean you lack faith; it means loss has changed everything. God meets you right where your harp hangs untouched. He stays with you, even when you cannot sing.

DAILY PRAYERS

DAY 1 God, I miss who I was before my child died. I miss feeling light, hopeful, and put together. This version of me feels unfamiliar and heavy. Please sit with me as I grieve not only my child, but the woman I used to be. Help me feel less alone in this loss. Amen.

DAY 2 Lord, the world expects me to be okay—to smile, to function like nothing shattered. I don't have the energy for that. Will you help me stop pretending? Give me permission to be honest about how hard this life feels and remind me I don't owe anyone a performance. Amen.

DAY 3 Father, I don't want this life without my child in it. I don't know how to live here, and I'm angry that this is part of my story now. Please let me bring everything I feel to you without filtering it. Stay close while I let it spill out. Amen.

DAY 4 God, I feel displaced inside my own life. Nothing fits the way it used to. When I feel pressure to celebrate a version of me I never wanted to become, remind me that you don't rush my heart. Meet me right where I am, even when joy feels out of reach. Amen.

DAY 5 God, I miss the person I was before my child died. I miss how life felt then, how *I* felt then. This version of me is unfamiliar and heavy. Please sit with me as I grieve this loss, too. Help me be gentle with who I am becoming. Amen.

DAY 6 Father, I'm tired of being told I'll adjust, that I'll find my way. I don't want to adjust to this life. Please stay with me while I learn how to exist here anyway. Help me breathe through today without asking more of myself than I can give. Amen.

DAY 7 God, as I face another week, I still don't know how to live this life without my child. But I'm here, and I'm being honest. Please remain close to me in this foreign place. When I struggle to sing and smile, stay with me anyway. Amen.

WEEK 36

Honoring Special Days and Anniversaries

Making space to remember without apology

But then I recall all you have done, O Lord;
I remember your wonderful deeds of long ago.
They are constantly in my thoughts.
I cannot stop thinking about your mighty works.

—Psalm 77:11–12

Anniversaries have a way of sneaking up on you. Birthdays, due dates, the day everything changed. While the world keeps moving, your body remembers. Your heart remembers.

Psalm 77 reminds us that remembering is not a failure of faith. It is the very act of it. The psalmist doesn't push memories away to survive. He brings them forward. He recalls. He reflects. He lets remembrance become part of how he walks with God.

After Gracie died, our family decided not to let those days pass quietly. On her birthday, I bake her a cake and invite others to wear pink. On the anniversary of her passing, we visit her ashes. These aren't rituals to stay stuck. They are ways of saying, *She mattered. She still matters.*

You may not know what honoring looks like for you yet. That's okay. It doesn't have to be public or perfect. Maybe it's having the barista write your child's name on your coffee cup to be called out. Buying them a new ornament for your tree every Christmas. Taking the day off work. Doing something meaningful with your body like walking, baking, creating, resting. Something that says, *I remember*.

There is no right way to mark these days. But pretending they don't exist often hurts more than acknowledging them.

God does not rush you past remembrance. He meets you in it. And honoring your child on these days is not dwelling on it in an unhealthy way. It is love continuing to speak.

DAILY PRAYERS

DAY 1 God, I don't always know how to honor my child in ways that feel right. Would you guide me as I figure that out? Help me notice what brings comfort instead of pressure. I don't need to do this perfectly, just honestly, in ways that fit my life. Amen.

DAY 2 Father, some days I want to plan ahead for the hard dates, and other days I can't even think about them. Can you meet me in both places? Give me wisdom to know when to prepare and when to rest. Help me trust that either choice can be loving. Amen.

DAY 3 God, I feel unsure about creating traditions. What if it hurts too much? What if it doesn't feel meaningful? Please take the fear out of trying. Show me one small way to remember my child that feels grounding instead of overwhelming. I'm open to learning as I go. Amen.

DAY 4 God, there's a day coming up that already feels heavy. Planning for it makes me anxious but not planning feels just as hard. Will you help me hold it with less fear? Give me peace before it arrives, clarity about what I need, and permission to do only what feels manageable. Amen.

DAY 5 God, I don't want honoring my child to feel performative or forced. I want it to feel real. Please help me release expectations about what remembrance should look like. Give me the freedom to honor them quietly, privately, or in different ways as my needs change. Amen.

DAY 6 Father, sometimes I feel pressure to mark every date, every milestone, every loss. It's exhausting. Help me discern what matters most to my heart. Remind me that remembering my child is not measured by how much I do, but by how deeply I love. Amen.

DAY 7 God, thank you for walking with me as I learn how to carry my child's memory through the years. I don't have it all figured out, and that's okay. Please continue to guide me gently, giving me ideas, strength, and permission to honor them in ways that fit who I am becoming. Amen.

How Do I Trust Myself Again?

Relearning how to trust myself after everything changed

He will not crush the weakest reed
or put out a flickering candle.
He will bring justice to all who have been wronged.

—Isaiah 42:3

After loss, it's not just your faith that takes a hit. Your trust in *yourself* does, too.

Perhaps you stop trusting your instincts because the worst thing already happened. Your nervous system is on high alert. Decisions that used to feel simple now feel loaded. Going back to work. Saying yes to plans. Making choices for your future. Everything feels risky—like one wrong move could break what's barely holding you together.

So you freeze. Or you second-guess every step. Or you wait for someone else to tell you what to do, because trusting your own heart feels hard now.

God doesn't shame fragility. He protects it. A bruised reed isn't discarded. A dim flame isn't extinguished. God treats what's tender with care. And that includes *you* while you relearn how to trust yourself again.

Here's the truth that grief makes hard to believe: The part of you that loves deeply didn't fail. Your instincts weren't wrong. Your heart wasn't careless. Loss does not mean you can't be trusted. It means you loved.

Rebuilding self-trust doesn't happen in big leaps. It happens in small, quiet decisions. Choosing rest when your body says "stop." Saying no without explaining. Taking one step forward, then pausing when you need to. Listening to the ache instead of fighting it.

Each time you honor what you feel instead of overriding it, you prove something to yourself: *I am allowed to listen to me again.*

The next time you feel God whisper, "Trust me, you can do this," trust yourself that you heard him right. God is not rushing you. He is guarding what's fragile while you learn, slowly, how to stand again.

DAILY PRAYERS

DAY 1 God, I don't trust myself the way I used to. Loss shook my instincts and made me doubt every decision. Can you meet me here and remind me that I'm not broken? Help me take today one small step at a time without fear. Amen.

DAY 2 Father, making choices feels overwhelming right now. Even simple decisions feel heavy. Will you sit with me as I learn to listen to my heart again? Help me know that moving slowly doesn't mean I'm failing. It means I'm being careful with what still hurts. Amen.

DAY 3 God, I used to trust my gut, but now I question everything. Is it okay that I don't know what I'm doing yet? Please steady me when doubt takes over and remind me that I'm allowed to learn again, even after all I've lost. Amen.

DAY 4 Lord, grief has paralyzed me. I hesitate because everything feels risky now. Will you walk with me as I learn to choose again? Help me trust that I'm allowed to move gently and that you are present even when I'm unsure. Amen.

DAY 5 Father, I feel disconnected from my own wisdom. I second-guess myself constantly. Can you help me recognize when my heart is speaking, not fear? I want to believe that I can still make decisions with care, love, and honesty. Amen.

DAY 6 God, some days I don't trust my thoughts, my feelings, or my reactions. Everything feels fragile. Please remind me that grief has shaped me, not erased me. Help me believe that I can still be gentle and trustworthy with my own life. Amen.

DAY 7 Lord, as this week ends, I'm still learning. I don't feel confident, but I'm here. Will you help me trust myself enough to take the next step, even if it's small? Thank you for staying close while I find my footing again. Amen.

WEEK 38

My Story Still Matters

Letting your story exist without fixing it

And they have defeated him by the blood of the Lamb
and by their testimony.
And they did not love their lives so much
that they were afraid to die.

—REVELATION 12:11

There was a season after Gracie died when I wondered if my story still mattered at all. Not just her story but mine. I wasn't the person people wanted to hear from anymore. My life didn't fit neatly into conversations. And over time, it became easier to stay quiet than to risk making someone uncomfortable.

Revelation 12:11 says, "They defeated him by the blood of the Lamb and by their testimony." That word testimony matters. It doesn't say by having the right answers. It doesn't say by being healed, hopeful, or polished. It says by telling the truth.

Your story matters because it's real; you lived it. There is power in saying, "This happened to me." Not to explain it. Not to justify it. Simply to refuse to erase it.

For a long time, I put pressure on myself to share my story only if it helped someone else. Only if it sounded hopeful enough. Only if it made sense. But your story doesn't exist to make other people comfortable. It exists because it's yours.

Telling your story doesn't mean you have to share everything, everywhere, with everyone. It might mean writing it down. Saying it out loud to God. Speaking it to one safe person. Or finally allowing yourself to admit, "This is part of who I am now."

Your story isn't over. And it hasn't lost its meaning just because it includes loss. God is not finished with you. Your voice still carries weight, even if it trembles when you use it.

DAILY PRAYERS

DAY 1 God, some days I honestly wonder if my story still has a place. Losing my child changed everything, including how I see myself. Will you help me believe that my life still matters, even when I feel erased? I want to trust that my voice still counts. Amen.

DAY 2 Father, I feel pressure to explain my story in ways that don't make people uncomfortable. I'm tired of editing my truth. When is it safe to be honest? Help me know when to speak and when to protect my heart, without feeling ashamed either way. Amen.

DAY 3 God, your Word says testimony has power, but I struggle to believe that includes mine. Does my story still matter even when it's messy and unresolved? Help me sit with that question. Show me that truth doesn't lose value just because it hurts. Amen.

DAY 4 Lord, there are days I feel invisible, like what I've lived through doesn't count anymore. Will you remind me that you see every part of my life, even the parts no one else acknowledges? Help me trust that nothing I've walked through has erased my worth. Amen.

DAY 5 Father, sharing my story feels vulnerable and exhausting. Some days I don't have the strength to explain myself. Give me grace to take this at my own pace. Teach me that I don't have to be brave or articulate for my story to matter. Amen.

DAY 6 God, I carry my child with me in ways no one else can see. Does that still count as something sacred? Help me believe that my love, my memory, and my truth hold weight, even when they live quietly inside me. Amen.

DAY 7 Lord, thank you for staying with me as I learn how to live with this story. I don't know what it's meant for yet, but I trust that you're not finished with me. Help me believe that my voice still matters, even here. Amen.

Learning to Live with the Ache That Stays

When healing doesn't mean the ache disappears

For no one is abandoned
by the Lord forever.
Though he brings grief, he also shows compassion
because of the greatness of his unfailing love.
For he does not enjoy hurting people
or causing them sorrow.

—Lamentations 3:31–33

There is a moment in grief when you realize the ache isn't going away. Not because you aren't healing, and not because you're doing something wrong, but because love doesn't disappear just because the person you love isn't here. That realization can feel discouraging, even frightening. You wonder: *Is this how I'll feel forever?*

Lamentations 3:31–33 speaks directly into that fear. These words were written in the middle of devastation, not after it passed. They don't deny the grief. They sit inside it.

This passage doesn't promise that sorrow will suddenly lift. It promises something steadier. You are not abandoned. Not now. Not later. Not in the long years of missing your child. God's compassion does not depend on your pain resolving. It meets you while the ache is still causing you pain.

Living with an ache that stays does not mean you've failed to move forward. It means you are carrying love in a different form. Some days the ache is quiet. Other days, it is loud and demanding. Neither is wrong. Both are part of learning how to live in a world that no longer looks the way it should.

God does not enjoy your suffering. He is not asking you to be okay with it. He is asking you to let him stay close while you learn how to live alongside it. The ache staying is not the absence of healing. It is the evidence of a love that never stopped.

DAILY PRAYERS

DAY 1 God, I'm realizing this ache isn't fading the way I hoped it would. Some days, that scares me. Help me understand that carrying this pain doesn't mean I'm failing. Teach me how to live with what remains instead of fighting it every moment. Stay close to me today. Amen.

DAY 2 Father, I miss my child in ways that don't go away. The love is still here and so is the loss. Is it okay that both exist at the same time? Help me stop judging myself for the weight I carry and remind me that you are not disappointed in me. Amen.

DAY 3 God, there are days when the ache feels manageable and days when it takes my breath away. I don't know which version of myself will wake up tomorrow. Please meet me in both. Help me trust that your compassion doesn't run out when my grief resurfaces. Amen.

DAY 4 Lord, I'm tired of wondering if this pain means something is wrong with me. I loved deeply, and now I hurt deeply. Help me accept that this ache is part of loving my child, not a sign that I'm stuck. Hold me steady when it feels heavy. Amen.

DAY 5 Father, you say you do not enjoy causing sorrow. I need to remember that today. When the ache convinces me you've abandoned me, gently remind me that you are still here, still compassionate, still near, even when the pain feels familiar and long-lasting. Amen.

DAY 6 God, people keep telling me it will get easier with time, and I don't know how to respond because it doesn't feel true. The ache hasn't faded; it's just changed. Help me to stop measuring my grief by other people's expectations. Remind me that there's no timeline for loving my child. Amen.

DAY 7 God, as I step into another week carrying this ache, I need to know I'm not doing it alone. Loving my child still hurts, and that hasn't changed. Please stay with me in the living, in the remembering, in all the days that come next. Hold me steady. Amen.

PART 4

Light After the Valley: Walking Toward Healing and Hope

WEEK 40

When Hope Feels Possible Again

Holding on to hope while waiting for what hasn't come yet

We were given this hope when we were saved. (If we already have something, we don't need to hope for it. But if we look forward to something we don't yet have, we must wait patiently and confidently.)

—Romans 8:24–25

Hope after child loss is not about believing life will feel better someday. For many mothers, hope becomes something far more specific and far more fragile. It is the belief that this separation is not permanent. That death did not get the final word. That you will see your child again.

Paul tells us that hope exists precisely because we do not have what we long for yet. If we already had it, we wouldn't need hope. That matters for grieving mothers because what we want most is not relief from pain. It's reunion. And that hope is future-facing by nature.

Waiting is woven into this verse. Not passive waiting but the kind that keeps breathing, keeps showing up, keeps trusting that God is still holding both you and your child. You may not feel strong while you wait. Sometimes waiting simply means you are still here, taking one more step forward.

For me, hope looks like this: I am still here because God is not finished with me yet. And I keep going because the story does not end here. Heaven matters now in a way it never did before. The promise that I will be reunited with my child is not an escape from this life—it's the anchor that keeps me in it.

Hope doesn't erase grief. It gives grief somewhere to rest. And while waiting is hard, Scripture reminds us that waiting itself is not wasted. God is present in it, holding the promises that have not yet been fulfilled.

DAILY PRAYERS

DAY 1 God, hope feels risky after everything I've lost. Part of me wants to hold it, and part of me wants to push it away. Can you meet me right here, in between? Help me trust that hoping doesn't mean forgetting my child or pretending I'm okay. Amen.

DAY 2 Father, waiting is exhausting. I want what I can't have yet, and that ache never leaves. Will you sit with me while I wait? Remind me that waiting does not mean you are withholding love or that I am doing this wrong. Amen.

DAY 3 God, the promise of seeing my child again is what keeps me breathing some days. When the waiting feels unbearable, help me remember that this separation is not permanent. Hold my heart steady when the future feels far away. Amen.

DAY 4 Lord, some days hope shows up quietly, and other days it disappears. Is it okay that it comes and goes? Please remind me that my faith isn't measured by consistency but by my willingness to keep showing up. Stay close when hope feels fragile. Amen.

DAY 5 Father, I don't want to rush this season or pretend the pain is smaller than it is. Help me live faithfully in the waiting, even when I don't know how long it will last. Teach me how to keep going without forcing myself forward. Amen.

DAY 6 God, I am still here, even though I never imagined this life. Does that matter to you? Remind me that my presence here has purpose, even when it feels unclear. Hold me in the tension of loving heaven and living here. Amen.

DAY 7 Lord, as I move into another week, I carry both grief and hope together. Thank you for not asking me to choose between them. Help me wait with honesty, love deeply, and trust that you are holding both my child and me. Amen.

Beauty from Broken Ground

What comes after the ruins?

To all who mourn in Israel,
he will give a crown of beauty for ashes,
a joyous blessing instead of mourning,
festive praise instead of despair.
In their righteousness, they will be like great oaks
that the LORD has planted for his own glory.

—ISAIAH 61:3

This verse is often quoted too quickly, as if beauty automatically replaces ashes. But Isaiah isn't pretending the ashes never existed. He names them first. Ashes are what remain after something has burned all the way down. They are evidence of devastation.

After losing a child, many mothers live in the ashes. Life looks nothing like it once did. The future you imagined is gone, and what's left feels fragile and unfamiliar. When Scripture speaks of beauty here, it is not minimizing that loss. It is acknowledging that God meets us *in* what has been destroyed, not after we clean it up.

Beauty in this passage is not happiness. It's not meaning-making or silver linings. It's the quiet, unexpected ways God tends broken ground over time. It might look like a deeper compassion you didn't choose, a steadiness you didn't know you had, or moments of tenderness that exist alongside grief, not instead of it.

God does not rush this exchange. He doesn't demand that ashes disappear before beauty can appear. He doesn't ask you to move on or reframe your loss. He works slowly, patiently, honoring what has been burned while planting something new in the same soil.

If you are beginning to notice small signs of beauty again, that doesn't mean your grief is shrinking or that your child matters less. It means God is working in places that once felt lifeless. Beauty doesn't erase ashes. It grows beside them, rooted in love that remains.

DAILY PRAYERS

DAY 1 God, I'm standing in the midst of a life that feels burned down. Nothing looks the way it used to. If you are still working here, will you show me gently? Help me trust that ashes don't mean you're finished with me and my story. Amen.

DAY 2 Father, when people talk about beauty after loss, it feels impossible. What does beauty even mean now? Please meet me in the wreckage without rushing me. Let me rest in knowing you see exactly what has been lost. Amen.

DAY 3 God, if anything new is growing in this broken place, I can't see it yet. Is it okay to not notice beauty right now? Stay with me while I learn how to live in this unfamiliar landscape. Amen.

DAY 4 Lord, I didn't choose this ground or the pain that came with it. Help me believe that you can tend what feels ruined without asking me to pretend it's okay. Walk with me slowly as I learn to breathe again. Amen.

DAY 5 God, today everything still feels heavy and unchanged. If there is any beauty here, will you help me notice it without forcing it? I'm not looking for answers or meaning, just a small reminder that you are present in this broken place. Amen.

DAY 6 God, I worry that noticing beauty means I'm leaving my child behind. Will you reassure me that love doesn't disappear when something new begins to grow? Hold my heart steady when those fears rise. Amen.

DAY 7 Lord, as this week ends, I'm still surrounded by ashes. Thank you for not asking me to clear them away. If beauty is coming, let it arrive in its own time. Stay near while I learn to live here. Amen.

WEEK 42

Learning to Smile Without Guilt

Releasing guilt around moments of joy

A time to cry and a time to laugh.
A time to grieve and a time to dance.

—Ecclesiastes 3:4

After loss, smiling again can feel complicated. You might catch yourself laughing and immediately feel it—the guilt. *Should I be doing this? Does this mean I'm moving on?*

I remember the first time I laughed after Gracie died. It caught me completely off guard. It felt like betrayal—like I had crossed some invisible line I wasn't supposed to cross. I remember thinking, *How can I laugh when my child is gone?*

Ecclesiastes doesn't rush us past grief, and it doesn't scold us for joy. It simply tells the truth: Life holds more than one season at a time. Crying and laughing aren't opposites. They exist side by side.

Grief doesn't end before joy begins. And joy doesn't cancel grief. You can miss your child deeply and still smile at a moment of beauty. One does not betray the other.

When joy comes unexpectedly, it can feel like you're breaking some unspoken rule—like you're supposed to stay sad in order to prove your love.

But love isn't measured by how long you stay miserable. Love is measured by how deeply your child mattered. And that doesn't disappear when joy sneaks in.

God is not surprised by your laughter. He is not offended by your smile. He doesn't see joy as disloyalty. He sees it as part of the life you are still living—a life that carries grief, memory, love, and yes, moments of light.

If you smiled today, you didn't forget your child. You simply stepped into a moment God allowed—and that's not something you need to apologize for.

DAILY PRAYERS

DAY 1 God, even the idea of joy feels complicated right now. Part of me wants relief, and part of me is afraid of what it would mean if I felt lighter. Please meet me exactly where I am today. Help me trust that joy, when it comes, doesn't erase my love or my grief. Amen.

DAY 2 Lord, I miss my child in every moment, even the lighter ones. When happiness surprises me, I freeze. Am I doing grief wrong? Please help me trust that joy doesn't erase love. Teach my heart that I can carry both without betraying either. Amen.

DAY 3 God, sometimes I stop myself from smiling because it feels safer to stay sad. What am I afraid of losing if I let joy in? Please meet me in this tension and show me that laughter doesn't take anything away from my child or my grief. Amen.

DAY 4 Father, when others see me smile, I worry they'll assume I'm okay. I'm not. I'm still grieving. Help me remember that joy doesn't mean I'm healed or finished hurting. It just means I'm still alive. Sit with me in both truths today. Amen.

DAY 5 God, I don't want to punish myself for moments of light. Please help me notice joy without bracing for shame afterward. If I find myself smiling today, help me receive it gently, without questioning my love or loyalty to my child. Amen.

DAY 6 Lord, I feel guilty when joy comes easily for a moment, and grief follows right behind it. Is this how it will always be? Please help me stop fighting the rhythm of my heart and trust that you understand this duality better than I do. Amen.

DAY 7 God, thank you for not demanding one emotion from me. As this week ends, help me release the belief that sadness proves my love more than joy does. Teach me how to live honestly—grieving fully, loving deeply, and smiling when I feel like it—without shame. Amen.

When I See God's Hand in the Ordinary

Noticing God without looking for answers

Look at the birds. They don't plant or harvest or store food in barns, for your heavenly Father feeds them. And aren't you far more valuable to him than they are?

—Matthew 6:26

Jesus's words in Matthew 6 aren't dramatic. He doesn't point to miracles or signs in the sky. He points to birds—ordinary, unnoticed, doing what they've always done. And he says, *Look.* Not to escape your pain but to remember you're still being held inside it.

After loss, the ordinary can feel cruel. The world keeps spinning. Groceries still need buying. Laundry still piles up. And sometimes it feels offensive that God would show up in something so small when your grief is anything but. You want answers, not breadcrumbs.

But God often meets us in small ways that don't demand anything from us. Not belief. Not gratitude. Not a spiritual response. Just attention.

For me, it started slowly. A moment of quiet in the car. A verse that landed heavier than the others. A sunset that made me stop instead of scroll. These weren't meant to explain my loss. They didn't fix anything. They were reminders that I wasn't abandoned inside my ordinary days.

Seeing God's hand in the ordinary doesn't mean you suddenly feel better. It means you're beginning to notice that grief hasn't pushed him out of your life. He's still there, steady and present, even when nothing feels sacred anymore.

Jesus didn't say the birds never struggle. He said they're cared for. And that matters.

If today all you can manage is noticing one small thing that didn't hurt as much as the rest, that counts. God isn't asking you to find meaning in everything. Sometimes he's simply reminding you that you're still seen, still sustained, still held in the middle of an ordinary day.

DAILY PRAYERS

DAY 1 God, today feels painfully ordinary, and part of me resents that. Where are you in the middle of errands, noise, and survival? Help me notice you without forcing meaning. Just let me know I'm not walking through this day alone. Amen.

DAY 2 Lord, I'm tired of looking for you and feeling like I come up empty. If you're here, will you show me in a way my heart can handle today? I don't need big answers. I just need reassurance that you're still near. Amen.

DAY 3 God, grief makes everything feel heavy, even the small things. But if you're present here, too, help me see it. Open my eyes to one gentle moment today and help me receive it without guilt or suspicion. Amen.

DAY 4 Father, I don't want to miss you because I'm expecting something dramatic. Teach me how to recognize you in quiet ways. Are you still caring for me even when nothing feels sacred anymore? Help me trust that you are. Amen.

DAY 5 God, today didn't feel meaningful, but it didn't crush me, either. Is that you sustaining me? Help me see your care in my ability to keep going, even when the day feels unremarkable and my grief is still loud. Amen.

DAY 6 Lord, sometimes the ordinary feels offensive after all I've lost. If you're meeting me here, help me soften my heart enough to notice. I don't need explanations. I just want to know you haven't stepped away from my everyday life. Amen.

DAY 7 God, thank you for staying present in places I didn't expect. As I move into another week, help me keep my eyes open without pressure. Remind me that even ordinary days are held by you. Amen.

WEEK 44

I've Been Carrying More Than I Thought

When survival starts to feel like strength

He gives power to the weak
and strength to the powerless. . . .
But those who trust in the LORD will find new strength.
They will soar high on wings like eagles.
They will run and not grow weary.
They will walk and not faint.

—ISAIAH 40:29–31

There's a moment in grief that sneaks up on you. You're not healed. You're not "better." But you realize you're carrying more than you thought you could. You get through a hard conversation. You make it through a day that once would've flattened you. And afterward you think, *How did I do that?*

Isaiah writes to people who are worn down, not triumphant. He doesn't tell them to dig deeper or try harder. He says God gives power to the weak and strength to the powerless. Not to the ones who feel ready. To the ones who don't.

That matters, because grief doesn't suddenly lift and leave you strong. It slowly teaches your body and heart how to keep going even while the ache stays. You don't wake up one day feeling capable. You just notice, one day, that you survived something you didn't think you would.

When Isaiah says those who trust in the Lord will "find new strength," he isn't promising energy or optimism. He's describing a quiet strengthening that happens underneath the pain. Strength you didn't earn. Strength you didn't ask for. Strength that met you in your weakest moments.

This isn't about running ahead or soaring above your grief. It's about realizing you're still here. Still breathing. Still standing.

And maybe that's the holy moment this week—not joy yet, not purpose yet, but the simple truth that God has been carrying you more than you realized. You're not strong because you've overcome grief. You're strong because God keeps meeting you inside it.

DAILY PRAYERS

DAY 1 God, I don't feel strong, but somehow I'm still here. I don't know how I made it through today. Was that you carrying me? If so, thank you. Please keep holding me when I don't have it in me to hold myself. Amen.

DAY 2 Lord, I'm tired in ways that rest doesn't fix. My body and heart feel worn thin. You say you give strength to the weary—can you meet me here, exactly as I am, without asking me to be more than this? Amen.

DAY 3 God, I didn't think I could survive some of the moments I've already lived through. And yet, here I am. Help me notice the strength you've been quietly giving me, even when I still feel weak. Amen.

DAY 4 Father, I'm learning that strength doesn't look like confidence or courage. It looks like getting up again. Breathing again. Trying again. If that's enough for today, help me believe it's enough for you, too. Amen.

DAY 5 God, when I compare myself to who I used to be, I feel defeated. When I look at today, I feel exhausted. Can you help me see myself the way you do—not failing, just still being carried? Amen.

DAY 6 God, I've noticed that some days I've reached a point where I'm not just surviving anymore. I can breathe a little deeper. I can listen without falling apart. Could that be strength growing quietly inside me? And if one day you ask me to carry someone else for a moment, show me when and how. Amen.

DAY 7 God, as this week ends, I'm realizing something small but important: I didn't do this alone. Thank you for the strength I didn't know I had and couldn't create on my own. Please keep meeting me right where I am. Amen.

WEEK 45

Helping Others Through Their Pain

Offering the kind of comfort I once needed

He comforts us in all our troubles so that we can comfort others. When they are troubled, we will be able to give them the same comfort God has given us.

—2 Corinthians 1:4

This verse is often quoted as encouragement, but it can feel heavy if it's misunderstood. Paul isn't saying suffering happens *so* you can help others, as if pain is an assignment. He's saying comfort is learned inside suffering, not after it's resolved.

Most people will never know what it's like to lose a child. They mean well, but they don't understand what that experience is like. They don't know what to say, what not to say, or how long the ache really lasts. You do. Not because you're stronger, but because you've lived it.

After Gracie died, I slowly realized I could see grieving parents in a way others couldn't. I knew that advice wasn't needed. I knew silence could be kindness. I knew that the worst thing wasn't tears, it was being avoided. That understanding didn't come from healing. It came from loss.

That's what Paul is naming here. The comfort God gives you in your own pain becomes something you can offer to someone who is standing at the beginning of theirs. And you can help. Not because you have answers but because you remember what it felt like to need someone who didn't rush you, fix you, or disappear.

Helping others doesn't mean reliving your grief or being available all the time. It can be as small as saying, "I know this road," or sitting with someone when everyone else has moved on. God doesn't ask you to explain pain away. He invites you to meet it with honesty.

Comfort isn't something you manufacture. It's something you recognize when you see it.

DAILY PRAYERS

DAY 1 God, I don't feel equipped to help anyone, but I know what it's like to hurt deeply. If you want to use my story in any way, please do it gently. Help me recognize when presence matters more than words. Amen.

DAY 2 Lord, I remember what it felt like when people disappeared. If you place someone in my path who is hurting, help me not rush them or fix them. Teach me how to sit with pain the way you sit with mine. Amen.

DAY 3 Father, sometimes I wonder if my grief could ever matter beyond my own heart. Is this pain something you can use to comfort someone else? If so, show me when to lean in and when to rest. Amen.

DAY 4 God, I don't have answers, and I don't want to pretend I do. If comfort comes through honesty, help me be honest. Let my presence be enough when someone else is standing where I once stood. Amen.

DAY 5 Lord, I'm afraid of being overwhelmed if I help others. Please guard my heart. Help me give only what I have, not more. Remind me that caring doesn't mean carrying everything alone. Amen.

DAY 6 God, thank you for the people who stayed with me when I was hurting. If I can be that kind of person for someone else, even in a small way, give me the courage to show up without fear. Amen.

DAY 7 Father, I see now that comfort isn't something I earned. It's something you freely offer to me. Help me trust that you will guide when and how I offer that same comfort to others. I'm listening. Amen.

WEEK 46

Gratitude in the Grief

How could I ever be thankful for this?

Always be joyful. Never stop praying. Be thankful in all circumstances, for this is God's will for you who belong to Christ Jesus.

—1 THESSALONIANS 5:16–18

At first glance, this passage can feel impossible after loss. Always joyful? Thankful in all circumstances? For a grieving mother, those words can sound dismissive or even cruel. But Paul is not writing these words to people with easy lives. He's writing to believers living under persecution, loss, and uncertainty.

The key phrase here is not "be thankful *for* all circumstances," but "be thankful *in* all circumstances." That distinction matters deeply. Paul is not asking anyone to be grateful for suffering, death, or loss. He is saying that gratitude can exist alongside pain, not outside of it.

Gratitude in grief is not happiness. It's not positivity. It's not pretending things are okay. Sometimes it looks like acknowledging that God is still present, even when joy feels unreachable. Sometimes it's recognizing that prayer doesn't stop just because words run out. Sometimes it's simply staying connected when everything inside wants to shut down.

This passage isn't a command to feel something you don't feel. It's an invitation to stay tethered to God through whatever season you're in. Joy may be rare. Prayer may be messy. Gratitude may be quiet and incomplete. And that still counts.

For a grieving mother, gratitude might be as small as noticing strength you didn't know you had or finding compassion when you expected abandonment. It doesn't erase grief. It coexists with it.

God's will here is not emotional perfection. It's relationship. Staying connected. Even in sorrow.

DAILY PRAYERS

DAY 1 God, I don't know how to hold gratitude without feeling like I'm betraying my child. Please help me understand that noticing your mercy doesn't mean I'm minimizing my loss. Can you sit with me while I learn how to hold both grief and gratitude without forcing either one? Amen.

DAY 2 Lord, today I don't feel thankful. I feel tired and heavy. If gratitude is here at all, it's buried under sorrow. Will you meet me where I actually am and not where I think I should be? Remind me that honesty matters more to you than forced words. Amen.

DAY 3 Father, people tell me to "be grateful," but they don't know what this costs me. Help me release the pressure to perform gratitude for others. Teach me what it looks like to notice your compassion quietly, without pretending this pain is smaller than it is. Amen.

DAY 4 God, I can't thank you for the pain of losing my child. I just can't. But I want to believe you are still compassionate toward me. Can you show me mercy in small, gentle ways today so I can remember that you have not abandoned me, even in this grief? Amen.

DAY 5 Lord, some days the only gratitude I can find is that I survived another hour. If that's enough, help me trust it. Teach me that gratitude doesn't have to sound beautiful to be real. Let it be quiet, imperfect, and honest. Amen.

DAY 6 Father, I'm afraid an attitude of gratitude will make people think I'm "better," when I'm not. Protect my heart from misunderstanding. Help me recognize your kindness without feeling rushed toward healing. Let gratitude be something that steadies me, not something that erases what I've lost. Amen.

DAY 7 God, as this week ends, I still feel the weight of grief. Thank you for not asking me to let it go. Help me trust that your compassion remains, even when sorrow does, too. Can you walk with me into the days ahead, holding both what hurts and what sustains me? Amen.

Peace That Doesn't Need Answers

Finding peace without understanding

Don't worry about anything; instead, pray about everything. Tell God what you need, and thank him for all he has done. Then you will experience God's peace, which exceeds anything we can understand. His peace will guard your hearts and minds as you live in Christ Jesus.

—**Philippians 4:6–7**

For a grieving mother, these verses can feel unrealistic at first. Don't worry about anything? Pray about everything? When your child has died, worry feels constant and prayer can be exhausting. And peace can feel completely out of reach.

But Paul is not promising answers here. He never says God will explain what happened. He doesn't say your circumstances will make sense. What he promises is peace that "exceeds anything we can understand." In other words, peace that doesn't make any sense.

After loss, answers often never come. *Why my child? Why this way? Why now?* If peace required clarity, most grieving mothers would never experience it. This passage offers something different. A peace that guards your heart while the questions remain.

Paul says to tell God what you need. Not what you *should* need. Not what sounds faithful. What you *actually* need. Maybe that's rest. Maybe it's relief from racing thoughts. Maybe it's the strength to get through the next hour. Gratitude here isn't about being thankful for loss. It's about remembering that God has not disappeared, even now.

This kind of peace doesn't arrive all at once. It settles in slowly. It shows up as steadiness in the middle of chaos. As a breath that doesn't feel so tight. As the ability to sit with unanswered questions without being undone by them.

God's peace is not an explanation. It is protection. And for a grieving mother, that is enough for today. You owe the world nothing more.

DAILY PRAYERS

DAY 1 God, my mind keeps searching for answers you haven't given. I'm exhausted from the questions. Can you give me peace that doesn't require understanding today? Help my heart rest even while the *why* remains unanswered. Please guard me when my thoughts spiral. Amen.

DAY 2 Lord, I tell you what I need, but sometimes I don't even know how to name it. I just know I'm tired. Will you meet me in this uncertainty and quiet the noise inside me? Teach me how to receive your peace without demanding clarity. Amen.

DAY 3 Father, the questions come back at night when everything is quiet. Why my child? Why this pain? I don't expect answers right now. I just need you to steady me. Can you hold my heart when the wondering feels too heavy? Amen.

DAY 4 God, I want peace, but I keep thinking it means forgetting or moving on. Please show me that your peace doesn't erase my love or my grief. Let it simply help me breathe again, right where I am, with everything I'm carrying. Amen.

DAY 5 Lord, some days peace feels impossible. My body is tense; my thoughts won't slow down. Will you guard my heart the way you promise, even when I can't calm myself? Help me trust that your peace works quietly, not all at once. Amen.

DAY 6 Father, I keep trying to solve what can't be solved. What if I let go of that today? What if peace isn't about answers at all? Please teach me how to rest in your presence without needing everything to make sense. Amen.

DAY 7 God, as this week ends, my questions are still there, but so are you. Thank you for peace that doesn't demand resolution. Will you continue to protect my heart as I live with what I don't understand? Stay with me in the waiting. Amen.

WEEK 48

The Strength to Keep Going

Leaning on God when I've reached my limit

Each time he said, "My grace is all you need.
My power works best in weakness." So now I
am glad to boast about my weaknesses, so that
the power of Christ can work through me. . . .
For when I am weak, then I am strong.

—2 CORINTHIANS 12:9–10

When we hear the word *strength*, we often imagine energy, confidence, resilience—the ability to keep going without falling apart. But Paul offers a different definition. In this passage, he admits he begged God to remove something painful from his life. God didn't. Instead, he answered with this: "My grace is all you need."

After your child died, strength probably didn't feel like bravery. It felt like waking up even when you didn't want to. Breathing through another day. Holding yourself together just long enough to function. You probably didn't feel powerful—you felt undone. And yet, here you are.

Paul doesn't pretend weakness is admirable. He names it plainly. He admits limits. He doesn't claim victory—he claims dependence. God meets him not when he overcomes, but when he is depleted. That's when this verse speaks to you.

The strength to keep going isn't about pushing harder or being tougher. It's about being carried when you have nothing left to give. God's grace doesn't wait for you to feel capable. It shows up in the middle of exhaustion, numbness, and doubt.

If you're still here, still breathing, still loving your child—even through tears—that is not failure. That is grace at work.

You don't need to prove your strength. You don't need to feel strong. God's power is already meeting you in the places you feel most depleted.

And for today, that is enough. *You* are enough.

DAILY PRAYERS

DAY 1 God, I feel so weak right now. I'm not sure how to keep going, and I don't want to pretend to be strong. Let your grace be enough for me today. Help me trust that you meet me in my weakness. Amen.

DAY 2 Lord, I'm exhausted from trying to hold everything together. Remind me that I don't have to. When I'm empty, fill me with your strength. Let me lean on you instead of my own efforts. Amen.

DAY 3 Father, sometimes I feel like I should be stronger by now. Remind me that your power shows up best in my weakness. I don't have to earn it. Thank you for being my strength when I have none left. Amen.

DAY 4 God, it's hard to admit that I'm struggling. You see it anyway. Help me be honest with you and let your grace hold me up. I don't have to be strong alone. Amen.

DAY 5 Lord, I'm afraid of feeling weak, as if it means I'm failing. Show me that it's okay to rest in your arms. Let me find peace in knowing that your grace is enough for this moment. Amen.

DAY 6 Father, when I feel like I can't take another step, remind me that you are carrying me. I don't have to figure everything out. I just need to lean on you. Thank you for being my strength. Amen.

DAY 7 God, as I face another week, let me remember that I don't walk alone. Your grace is my strength. Your presence is my comfort. Help me trust that even my smallest steps are held by you. Amen.

Living Fully Without Letting Go

Making room for life without releasing love

Now we see things imperfectly, like puzzling reflections in a mirror, but then we will see everything with perfect clarity. All that I know now is partial and incomplete, but then I will know everything completely, just as God now knows me completely. Three things will last forever—faith, hope, and love—and the greatest of these is love.

—1 CORINTHIANS 13:12–13

After losing a child, living fully can feel impossible—or even wrong. Loving deeply might feel dangerous now, like it could cost you everything again. You didn't choose to become cautious; grief taught you how fragile life can be.

Paul's words meet us right there. He doesn't pretend we understand things clearly now. He admits we see imperfectly. We don't know why some lives are short. We don't know how joy and sorrow are supposed to coexist. That confusion isn't failure—it's part of living in the in-between.

What Paul does make clear is this: Love remains.

Your love for your child didn't end when they died. And choosing to live fully now doesn't erase that love—it flows from it. Loving deeply after loss looks different. It's softer. More intentional. Less rushed. You notice people more. You feel more. You carry both tenderness and ache at the same time.

Living fully doesn't mean pretending you're okay. It means allowing life to keep moving through you while love stays anchored to what mattered most. It means showing up honestly—with grief still present—and letting love guide how you live now.

Faith may feel fragile. Hope may come and go. But love never stopped. It shaped you as a mother, and it continues to shape the way you live.

You are not betraying your child by choosing to live. You are honoring them by letting love still have a voice in your life—here, now, and always.

DAILY PRAYERS

DAY 1 God, I'm learning to live fully again, but it feels like walking on new ground. Help me trust that loving deeply doesn't erase my grief—it honors it. Let love find its way in me. Amen.

DAY 2 Lord, sometimes I'm afraid to embrace life fully because it feels like I'm leaving my child behind. Remind me that loving deeply now doesn't diminish my love for them. They're part of this journey, always. Amen.

DAY 3 Lord, when I struggle to believe that living fully is okay, remind me that you created me for love. You're not asking me to forget my child, but to carry their love forward as I live. Amen.

DAY 4 Father, I need the courage to live fully, even when it feels vulnerable. Help me trust that each step I take is held by you. Let love be the reason I keep going. Amen.

DAY 5 God, I don't know what "fully alive" looks like for me now. My life feels smaller, quieter, different. Can you help me trust that this version of me still matters? That my presence here still has meaning? Amen.

DAY 6 Father, help me say yes to small things again. Small plans. Small hopes. Small steps forward. I don't need a big vision right now. Just enough strength to stay engaged with the life in front of me. Amen.

DAY 7 God, as this week ends, help me see that living fully and loving deeply is not a betrayal of my grief—it's a testament to it. Thank you for walking with me through both loss and love. Amen.

WEEK 50

Letting Go of the Need to Explain Myself

Releasing the need to be understood

Who are you to condemn someone else's servants? Their own master will judge whether they stand or fall. And with the Lord's help, they will stand and receive his approval.

—Romans 14:4

By a certain point in grief, something subtle but exhausting often settles in: the feeling that you still need to explain yourself. Why you grieve the way you do. Why certain things are still hard. Why you've made the choices you've made. Why your faith looks different now.

No one's asking outright anymore, but you can feel it. The unspoken expectations. The raised eyebrows. The quiet judgments. And without realizing it, you're narrating your life to make it more comfortable for others.

Romans 14:4 disrupts that expectation. Paul is speaking to a community where people were constantly evaluating each other's choices. His words are clear: You are not accountable to everyone's opinion. You belong to God. And he is the one who sustains you.

Grief teaches you this slowly, and often painfully. At first, you explain because you're trying to survive. You soften your truth. You justify your boundaries. You clarify your decisions. But over time, that constant explaining becomes its own burden.

Letting go of the need to explain yourself is not bitterness. It's maturity. It's trusting that God sees your heart without footnotes. It's realizing that your life, your grief, and your healing don't need a defense.

You are allowed to live quietly. You are allowed to change. You are allowed to stop translating your pain for people who aren't meant to carry it.

God is not confused by your story. He is not disappointed by your pace. You don't need to convince anyone else of what he already knows.

DAILY PRAYERS

DAY 1 God, I'm tired of explaining myself. Tired of justifying my grief, my choices, my limits. Will you help me rest in the truth that you already understand me fully? Teach me that I don't owe clarity to everyone when my heart is already carrying so much. Amen.

DAY 2 Lord, sometimes I feel watched, measured, quietly judged. I don't always know how to respond. Do I defend myself or stay silent? Please give me wisdom to know when to speak and courage to let silence be enough when words would only drain me. Amen.

DAY 3 Father, I keep trying to make my story easier for others to hear. Why do I do that? Help me trust that my life doesn't need to be minimized to be valid. Teach me how to live honestly without apologizing for the shape grief has given me. Amen.

DAY 4 God, there are days I rehearse explanations in my head before conversations even happen. Will you help me release that habit? Remind me that you are my witness, my defender, my steady ground when I feel unsure of how I'm being perceived. Amen.

DAY 5 Lord, I want to stop carrying the weight of other people's expectations. Show me where I've taken on pressure you never placed on me. Help me loosen my grip on approval and may I trust that your understanding is enough to hold me steady. Amen.

DAY 6 God, when I feel misunderstood, I want to fix it immediately. Why does that feel so urgent? Teach me that not being understood doesn't mean I'm doing something wrong. Help me stay rooted in truth instead of constantly reaching for reassurance. Amen.

DAY 7 Father, as I move forward, help me live with less explaining and more peace. Let me trust that the people who are meant to walk with me will not require constant justification. And when they don't understand, remind me that you do, fully and completely. Amen.

A Faith That Endures

Staying when the miracle didn't come

All these people died still believing what God had promised them. They did not receive what was promised, but they saw it all from a distance and welcomed it.

—**Hebrews 11:13**

I used to think enduring faith meant eventually getting the miracle. That if you believed long enough or hard enough, the story would turn out right.

But thirteen years after Gracie died, I still walk into church and see videos of families who got their miracle. The baby lived. The prayer was answered. The story all wrapped up with hope and applause. And if I'm honest, sometimes I get sick of it. Not because I'm bitter toward them but because I asked for a miracle, too. And stories like mine, the ones where the miracle didn't come, are rarely told.

Hebrews 11 reframes faith completely. The men and women mentioned in this chapter didn't receive what they hoped for. They didn't see the promise fulfilled in their lifetime. And yet Scripture calls them faithful. Not because they got the ending they wanted but because they stayed connected to God anyway.

Faith does not come *after* a miracle. Faith is what carries you when the miracle doesn't happen. It's what keeps you standing in rooms where other people's prayers were answered and yours still ache. It allows you to keep loving God without pretending the disappointment isn't there.

Enduring faith is not cheerful or polished. It's quiet, worn, and often full of questions. It's choosing to keep walking with God even when your story didn't turn out the way you begged it to.

And according to Scripture, that kind of faith is not lesser. It is named. It is honored. And it lasts.

DAILY PRAYERS

DAY 1 God, I'm still here, even when my faith feels thin. I didn't get the miracle I prayed for, but I haven't walked away, either. Does that count as faith? Please meet me in this quiet endurance and remind me that staying still matters, too. Amen.

DAY 2 Lord, I see stories of answered prayers everywhere, and sometimes it hurts more than it helps. Where do I put the grief of prayers you didn't answer? Help me believe that my faith still matters, even without applause, even without resolution. Amen.

DAY 3 God, some days my faith doesn't feel strong or sure. It feels quiet and tired. I'm still choosing to stay, even when nothing has changed. Can you meet me here, exactly as I am, without asking for more than I have today? Amen.

DAY 4 Father, I carry both trust and disappointment in the same heart. I didn't receive what I begged you for, and yet I keep coming back. How do you see this kind of faith? Teach me that endurance is not failure, even when the miracle didn't come. Amen.

DAY 5 God, some days my faith looks like silence, not praise. It looks like showing up without understanding. Do you still call that faith? Help me believe that walking forward without answers is still a form of trust. Amen.

DAY 6 God, I'm still here, even though this road hasn't looked like I hoped. Some days I don't know what I believe, only that I haven't walked away. Can you meet me where I am, without asking me to explain it or dress it up? Amen.

DAY 7 God, thank you for holding me through another week. I didn't get the miracle, but I'm still here, still believing, still reaching for you. If this is what enduring faith looks like, help me keep going. I need you. Amen.

WEEK 52

Joy Comes with the Morning (and in the Mourning)

Joy that doesn't erase grief

Sing to the LORD, all you godly ones!
Praise his holy name.
For his anger lasts only a moment,
but his favor lasts a lifetime!
Weeping may last through the night,
but joy comes with the morning.

—PSALM 30:4–5

This verse is often quoted like a promise that pain has an expiration date. Like if you just hold on long enough, grief will politely step aside and joy will replace it. That's not how mourning works after child loss.

Psalm 30 wasn't written by someone who avoided suffering. David knew grief, fear, loss, and waiting. When he writes about weeping in the night, he isn't minimizing it. He's naming it. The night can last a long time. Sometimes much longer than we expect. Sometimes stretching into years.

Joy doesn't mean happiness or forgetting. It doesn't mean the pain disappears. It means that grief is no longer the only thing that lives inside you. Joy is moments where light shows up alongside the ache, not instead of it.

After Gracie died, joy felt impossible. And honestly, offensive. How could joy exist in a world where my child didn't? What I've learned over the years is that joy didn't come to replace grief. It came to live with it.

Joy looked like laughing, then crying five minutes later. It looked like warmth in my chest followed by the familiar ache. It looked like loving deeply again without betraying the child I lost.

This is what "joy comes with the morning" means—and by extension, the mourning. Not that the night didn't matter. Not that the night didn't change you. But that the night doesn't get the final word.

You don't have to chase joy. You don't have to force it. And you don't have to feel it every day.

Joy comes quietly. Gently. On grief's terms. And when it does, it doesn't erase your mourning. It honors it.

DAILY PRAYERS

DAY 1 God, the night has been long. Some days it still feels endless. I don't need you to rush me into joy. I just need to know you're here with me in the dark, not waiting on the other side of it. Amen.

DAY 2 Father, when joy shows up quietly, I don't always know what to do with it. Part of me is afraid it means I'm leaving my child behind. Please remind me that joy doesn't erase love. It doesn't replace grief. It can live alongside it. Amen.

DAY 3 God, some mornings feel lighter and others don't. When my emotions shift, I wonder if my faith is shifting, too. Remind me that feelings rise and fall, but you remain. Help me stop measuring my faith by how heavy or light today feels. Amen.

DAY 4 Lord, I still carry sorrow in my body. I still miss my child deeply. And yet, sometimes I laugh or feel warmth again. Help me stop questioning whether that's allowed. Let joy be a companion, not a contradiction, to my love. Amen.

DAY 5 God, I don't want joy that pretends nothing happened. I want the kind that knows my story and still stays. If joy comes today, help me receive it without guilt. And if it doesn't, help me trust that I'm still okay. Amen.

DAY 6 Father, mourning has become part of my life, and some days it still feels too heavy to hold. Some days I feel numb, other days overwhelmed. Please meet me exactly where I am today. I don't need answers. I just need you to stay with me here. Amen.

DAY 7 God, thank you for walking with me through every week, every ache, every breath. My joy isn't loud or complete, but it's real. Help me trust that this quiet, fragile joy is enough for today. Stay with me as I keep saying yes to life. Amen.

Acknowledgments

First, to my Savior—thank you for meeting me on these pages before they ever met a reader. For the words I didn't know how to say, the Scriptures that rose up when mine fell short. This book belonged to you long before it belonged to me.

To my spouse and family—thank you for your patience and the countless ways you held down the fort while I disappeared into words and deadlines. Thank you for the sacrificed time, the grace on the hard days, and for loving me well when writing asked more of me than I expected. I couldn't have done this without you—and I wouldn't want to.

To my editors, Patty and Kim—thank you for your constant encouragement and for gently (and sometimes not so gently) pulling more out of me than I planned to give. Especially the anger. The things my Minnesota niceness prefers to tuck away neatly and pretend don't exist. Thank you for making this book braver, truer, and deeper.

And to the team at Zeitgeist and Penguin Random House—thank you for seeing a need—and trusting me to help meet it. I didn't bring this devotional to you; you found me and invited me into this work, and I don't take that lightly. Thank you for believing in this book, this voice, and for the care you brought every step of the way.

This book was not written alone—and I am thankful for every hand, heart, and holy nudge that helped bring it into the world.

About the Author

Becky Hunt is a mother, author, and speaker who writes for those navigating grief while still longing for God.

She is the author of *Joy Does Return: How God Meets You in Your Grief and Restores the Joy You Thought Was Gone*, a book shaped by the long, complicated road that followed losing her daughter, Gracie—one marked by deep grief, hard questions about God, cancer survival, autoimmune diseases, and the slow, brave work of choosing to keep living. Her writing offers companionship rather than answers—faith-filled honesty for those walking through sorrow without a map.

Becky is also the host of the podcast *Loud About Loss*, where she creates space for honest conversations about grief, faith, and life after loss—especially the parts that often go unspoken. Through both her writing and speaking, Becky hopes others feel less alone and more free to bring their whole, unfiltered hearts before God.

Through this devotional, Becky hopes to offer you a steady presence and a gentle reminder that you are not doing grief wrong. God is not threatened by your questions, and you do not have to rush healing to be faithful.

She lives in Minnesota with her husband and daughters and continues to believe that joy does not return by forgetting what was lost—but by learning how to live with love and grief side by side. Connect with her at beckyhunt.net.

Hi there,

We hope *I Am Near* serves as a source of connection and comfort for you. If you have any questions or concerns about your book, or have received a damaged copy, please contact customerservice@penguinrandomhouse.com. We're here and happy to help.

Sincerely,

The Zeitgeist Team